W9-DGV-009

LEFT FOR DEAD

*The Life, Death, and
Possible Resurrection of
Progressive Politics in America*

MICHAEL TOMASKY

THE FREE PRESS

New York   London   Toronto   Sydney   Singapore

THE FREE PRESS
A Division of Simon & Schuster Inc.
1230 Avenue of the Americas
New York, NY 10020

Copyright © 1996 by Michael Tomasky
All rights reserved,
including the right of reproduction
in whole or in part in any form.

THE FREE PRESS and colophon are trademarks
of Simon & Schuster Inc.

Designed by Carla Bolte

Manufactured in the United States of America

10 9 8 7 6 5 4 3 2 1

Library of Congress Cataloging-in-Publication Data

Tomasky, Michael.

 Left for dead: the life, death, and possible resurrection of
progressive politics in America / Michael Tomasky.

    p.   cm.

    ISBN 0-684-82750-6

    1. United States—Politics and government—1993–   2. United
States—Economic policy—1993–   3. United States—Social
policy—1993–   4. Progressivism (United States politics)
5. Liberalism—United States. 6. Conservatism—United States.

I. Title.

JK271.T66   1996   96–3825
973.929—dc20   CIP

For my parents,

MICHAEL AND MARY

keepers of family values that matter.

CONTENTS

ACKNOWLEDGMENTS

I'll keep it short. Many people contributed to the making of this book. Dozens of colleagues, journalists, friends, politicians, and others have been good enough to sit down with me and engage in discussions on the topics this book covers, offering their thoughts and ideas. Some of these conversations took place in the specific context of my work on this book, and some did not; all were valuable. Several friends read portions of the manuscript. You know who you are. Each of these encounters made me think things through more fully than I had. I thank all of you sincerely, and hasten to assure you that your input, however small or large, leaves you free to criticize, condemn, and rebuke to your heart's content.

They say that a writer should not hire a friend as an agent, but in my case, Chris Calhoun's wise support and enthusiasm shattered that weak piece of conventional wisdom. They also say that editors don't edit books anymore; I have in my possession the several letters and hundreds of Post-it notes proving that with respect to Mitch Horowitz, such is emphatically not the case. Phil Zabriskie provided valuable research assistance, and Valerie Burgher and Jennifer Gonnerman helped procure some needed documents. Finally, I'd like to thank Cecelia Cancellaro, who said to me, just after I wrote the essay that led to this book, that I should expand it to book length.

Introduction

BLEACHED BONES AND
JUMBLED RESIDUES

Not many Americans had the chance to be told, face to face, to prepare themselves for a different future. So in that, at least, I count myself fortunate. I was in Atlanta in October 1992 for the vice presidential debate, an event memorable only for Admiral James Stockdale's interesting performance. After the debate, an impromptu spin center had been set up in an adjacent ballroom in the building on the Georgia Tech campus where the encounter took place. Press aides to various politicians held placards high in the air with their bosses' names on them; to gather the various perfunctory reactions to the evening's proceedings, a reporter needed merely to walk the eight or so feet from the "Lewis" sign, where Georgia Congressman John Lewis held forth, over to the "Miller" sign, indicating the presence of Georgia's governor, and so on down the line.

1

After conversing with a few of the friendly ones—pols who I calculated would be more or less willing to pass a moment with a card-carrying representative of the *Village Voice*—I decided that I'd only be in such a situation once in the foreseeable future and so I might as well trundle over to the "Gingrich" sign. I'd called his office a couple of times since I'd gotten to town; calls that, to my total unsurprise, were not returned. But there the man stood, more or less by himself for a brief moment, so I pounced. Oh, yes, he said, I've been meaning to call you back. Love to talk to you. I'll be shaking hands at an office park tomorrow morning, and later in the day I have some downtime; maybe we can sit down at my campaign office. There's nothing more unnerving for the ideologically declared reporter than a politician from the enemy camp being charming, so I was suspicious in the extreme of his solicitude. But in all such instances, the reporter's curiosity defeats the partisan's suspicion, so off I went.

Sure enough, the next afternoon found us sitting in Gingrich's campaign office. He began by showing me some court papers relating to his opponent's personal life. This opponent was having fun in the local papers with the now well-known story of Gingrich's showing up at his first wife's hospital bed to discuss divorce terms, and Gingrich delightedly shared his planned counterpunch, which also had something to do, if memory serves, with family values found wanting. As the talk turned to presidential politics, I reminded him that he had counseled voters earlier in the campaign season to think of the contest as "a *Village Voice* versus *Reader's Digest* campaign"—a handy comparison for his side, since the *Digest*'s circulation is many dozens of times that of the *Voice*.

On and on it went, until finally I asked him about his own designs on the presidency. No, I have no great interest in that, he said; it's Speaker of the House that I'm after. I asked how soon he really thought he might be able to pull *that* one off. Six years, with a little luck maybe less, he said; and I remember rolling my eyes to the heavens as he said it.

Two years later, there I was in the ballroom of the Sheraton New York in midtown Manhattan, at the "victory" party of Mario Cuomo. The greatest liberal icon of his age, but in fact a mediocre to bad governor, Cuomo had faced his first serious challenge as incumbent that day. Very few Democrats, after 12 years, adored the man—most, earlier in the year, would have told you privately that they hoped he wouldn't run again—but most of them still expected him to win. He was, after all, something big, a national symbol, and this George Pataki fellow was an unknown, a real estate hustler from, for God's sake, Peekskill (never underestimate New York City parochialism). So victory was more or less expected, without enthusiasm for the incumbent but with anticipated relief that New Yorkers would swim, as they so pride themselves on doing, or thinking they do, against the tide.

Cuomo was erased before midnight. But that, of course, was not all the night held in store. On the ballroom floor, about 40 feet back from the stage, the media were gathered. Television cameras, 20 or 25 of them, were set up on risers, radio correspondents had a table off to the side, print reporters milled about. Naturally, where there are cameras and microphones there are politicians, and so state legislators, members of Congress, borough presidents, what have you, were out in abundance, making themselves available to all who sought their wisdom. It was in this press pit, sometime around 11 o'clock, that I saw Charles Schumer, the liberal Brooklyn congressman who had made no secret, earlier in the year, of his desire to run for governor if Cuomo bowed out (and who is not known to walk away from a working camera). Finally, here was someone who surely was keeping an eye on what was happening around the country tonight. This being a Cuomo affair, there was no official recognition in the room that anyone should be interested in any fate other than the governor's—no televisions tuned to CNN, nothing. I had been at the home of friends earlier that night and knew that, by barely 9 o'clock, Republican control of the Senate was already virtually assured. But results from House races were coming in more slowly. So what, I asked Schumer, have you heard?

It's bad, Schumer said. Meaning what? "Well," he continued, "I hear it could be as high as 50 seats." I thought back, at that moment, to my meeting with Newt at his campaign headquarters in a strip mall in suburban Atlanta. Well, I thought, one thing I can't say is that I wasn't warned.

It's useful to recall that the 54 House seats the Republicans did pick up to gain control of that body well exceeded most people's expectations. I'd tracked the consultants' and pundits' predictions closely, and most of them thought the GOP gain would be in the 20 to 40 range. The very few Republican consultants who predicted a 50-seat pickup seemed wildly optimistic, boastful, heedless. But even they, it turned out, sold their side short. The House results, combined with the seven-seat gain in the Senate, gave Republicans complete control of Congress for the first time in 40 years—the first time in my lifetime, certainly, and in the lifetimes of most of the people I knew. Even those who had been around were hard put to recall any House action taken under Joseph Martin, the last Republican speaker, so distant and obscure was the memory.

But the Republican ascendance hardly ended there. In statehouses, in state legislatures, on state referendums, at practically every level, Republicans triumphed. Or, to put it more precisely, the right triumphed, because among the big winners there were to be found almost none of that stripe disdainfully known today as "Rockefeller Republicans." So now, Pennsylvania had a Republican governor, a state legislature in which the GOP would end up controlling both houses, and a conservative new senator, Rick Santorum, who had defeated Harris Wofford, the man whose earlier victory had been seen as a mandate for national action on health care reform. Ohio, too, went Republican at all levels; the Democratic candidate for governor won a mere 28 percent of the vote, just three points above the minimum required to maintain the party's ballot status for the next four years. New York followed suit— Democrats maintained control of the State Assembly, but many upstate Democrats are somewhat conservative and besides, Pataki's victory meant the balance of power in state politics would shift away from the liberal big city. In Texas, a former president's son, positioned well to his father's right, dumped another liberal Democratic icon in Ann Richards. In California, the conservative governor rolled to reelection and voters easily passed a ballot initiative that cut off aid to immigrants in such a way as to be blatantly athwart all legal precedent. And on and on. Republicans now controlled the Senate, the House, 30 of 50 governors' mansions, 52 of 99 state legislative chambers, both chambers in 20 states, and more local offices than they had at any point since probably the 1920s.

This was paydirt of a sort the right couldn't have dreamed of hitting even in 1980. True, Ronald Reagan crushed Jimmy Carter that year, and Republicans took control of the Senate. But Republican control of presidential politics has been practically a given since 1968, with Carter, and now Clinton, seen mostly as aberrations, or as brief correctives to the sort of turpitude that sets in when one party controls something for too long—or, if you want to be less grandiose about it, as reasonable alternatives to two bumbling GOP incumbents. So Reagan's win was no surprise. Similarly, the 1980 Republican victory in the Senate, when the party picked up 12 seats, can be seen in retrospect as a function, in no small part, of Reagan's coattails, both personal and ideological. His message of limited government, fiscal restraint, and a stronger national defense was one Republicans had been pounding home for years, but it took a wrecked economy, a weakened Carter, and a charismatic Reagan to make it resonate beyond the presidential level. An inordinate number of Democratic senators representing basically conservative states—Frank Church of Idaho, John Culver of Iowa, Birch Bayh of Indiana—also didn't hurt. And it's true, too, that the GOP picked up 33 seats in the House of Representatives that year, but the House, the body whose composition remains the best reflection of the national political mood, was still Democratic by a 243 to 192 margin (even if those Democrats proved quiescent in the extreme in Reagan's first years). And the party of the working people, as it still fashioned itself, continued to control 27 governors' mansions and to conduct most of the nation's business at the state and local level. But 1994 was another matter altogether: the Senate, the House, the statehouses and state legislatures; surely had it been a presidential election year, the GOP would have taken the presidency, too. In 1994, more emphatically even than in 1980, Republican domination of presidential politics had filtered down to the lower levels, to the point that Democrats could be said to control politics only in a few smokestack cities and the Southern state legislatures, with the latter stronghold fading away fast. The Reagan revolution had finally beheld its real moment of victory.

But chalking up electoral winners and losers describes only the surface of the right's triumph, the way an atoll reveals only the top of the sprawling reef below. For people on the left, the activists and thinkers and others who had devoted themselves to the movements of the 1960s and '70s and their goals, seeing a bunch of played out liberals like Cuomo and Tom Foley and Dan Rostenkowski take it on the chin was not what rankled. What *was* troubling was that the '94 elections were the culmination of the victory of an ideology. Consider the world as it is explained today in most political conversation. White people, not the race of people who were enslaved for 250 years, are aggrieved; blacks enjoy special treatment. Government can do no good; only private enterprise, which, according to its laudators, is blameless, magically efficient, and free of all the perfidious forces that enfeeble the public sector, can rescue the country. The poor need discipline; people who make more than $200,000 a year need huge tax breaks. The Cold War is over, the enemy no longer exists; yet the Pentagon still needs gobs of money, just in case it has to fight two major wars at once (as if public opinion would support for any length of time two major wars at once!). Corporations are moving as many jobs, as quickly as they can, out of the cities and towns they've served for generations and into slave-wage countries; but what's needed aren't protections for American workers (and, God knows, not expansion of union rights) or agreements that will help equalize international wage structures, but more latitude for the beleaguered corporations. It's worth noting that this political landscape, with the exception of arguments over affirmative action and the size of tax breaks, is accepted as more or less sensible by most of the leaders of both major political parties. And most voters, who don't stay terribly well informed and who, after all, can only choose from what's on the menu, are buying this stuff. Worst of all, it's difficult to imagine a way out; it wasn't all that long ago, in historical terms, that the nation's goals were social justice and compassion toward the poor, and that even redistribution of the nation's wealth could at least be publicly discussed. Today, all of those are well outside the bounds of most political discussion, and nothing, it seems, will be changing very soon.

Even more exasperating, the right has managed to cloak this triumph of the few over the many in language that for more than a century had been *ours*: the language of community and aspiration. It is now the right that speaks of equality of opportunity and the dream of a colorblind society. It is the right that envisions, in its terse and cauterized way, an American nation built on the republic's founding principles of the Enlightenment. The right has even managed to appropriate the left's most noble imagery. In his maiden address as Speaker of the House, Newt Gingrich reminded his giddy Republican charges that, if it had been up to their party, there would have been no civil rights revolution in this country, and that Republicans owed a debt to the many brave people who made and supported that revolution. He's right, we're all in their debt, but given the obvious fact that Gingrich and his cohorts, had they been in the House then, would surely have done all they could to block civil rights (and, let's note, would have joined their Southern Democratic colleagues in doing so), it was hard to take that one with equanimity. But Gingrich's speech was effective, and the ashen faces of congressional liberals as Gingrich spoke those words brought home a sobering point: the only reason the right can use such rhetoric is that the left has abandoned it.

The usually deliberate pace of political events presents great changes in increments and, over time, makes everything seem normal to those watching closely. An infant grows; its parents see small changes daily, but it takes an infrequent visitor to see immediately how the child has changed. To have followed the right's triumph closely—to have read the newspapers and journals, talked to the people—is to have watched it evolve over time in a way that seems logical, expected. But to step back, to unlearn for a moment all that one has learned from the close monitoring of daily events, is to see in stark relief that the country has changed in ways that would have been unimaginable some years ago. How in the world did we get here?

We know many of the answers to that question. The prosperity of the 1950s and 1960s is long gone, and in an age of scarcity, people will fight savagely for their slice of the pie.

Many liberal programs built on the assumption of that prosperity were badly conceived or executed (one thinks, for example, of the antipoverty programs so open to corruption) or disastrously wrongheaded (court-mandated busing, which put working-class whites and poor blacks at war). A crafty right knew how to exploit those mistakes, and a somewhat worse than crafty right put racial fear at the center of its program. And of course, racism, sexism, and homophobia remain rampant, seemingly insurmountable obstacles to change. We on the left know and accept these explanations, and this ground has been thoroughly covered—to the exclusion of all other issues.

This book is an attempt to answer the part of the question that is, for those on the left, far and away the most difficult part to confront: where have *we* gone wrong? It's not a question many people on the left choose to contemplate. Writers, critics, and public figures on the left—and allow me for the moment to use the term broadly, as I feel it may permissibly be used in the post-Cold War era, to include everyone from the leading radical critics to the more liberal members of Congress; differences, which are important, will be detailed in a later chapter—have devoted much energy to assaying the right's goals and tactics. Pick up any issue of *The Nation, The Village Voice, Mother Jones, In These Times,* or *The Progressive* and you're likely to find a reasonably thoughtful critique of GOP welfare policy or a solid-enough taking apart of Phil Gramm. Read through the floor speeches of legislators like New York Congressman Major Owens or Minnesota Senator Paul Wellstone and you'll hear a voice that speaks up to defend the minimum-wage earner or the struggling single mother against the right's assaults. Watch the news and eventually you'll see Jesse Jackson pop up, criticizing the right on affirmative action or Medicare.

What you won't find much of in those journals, or hear much of from those people, though, is any attempt at self-

examination. It's easy to see why: to blame racism or a mendacious and manipulative right wing or a stupidly conservative
general public provides comfort, ratifies already held ideas
about how things are (and, not coincidentally, alleviates the
responsibility to make change). To examine one's own short-
comings is far more difficult. The left loves the idea of self-
examination but abhors its practice, because any serious
self-examination will show that the left is considered broadly
and laughably irrelevant by many people. And we have to ask
ourselves why. Examine our own ideas and programs, or lack
of them. Consider the intellectual underpinnings of much current left-wing thought, particularly as they relate to what we
call identity politics, and how those underpinnings fit and
don't fit with notions about a civil society that most Americans can support. Reflect on our rhetoric, strategies, policy
choices on issues like welfare, immigration, and affirmative
action, and why they're just not working. And no one, surely,
would attempt to make the case that they *are* working. We're
in our weakest position since the 1950s, maybe even since the
1920s, and are considered about as lively a threat to business
as usual as the Trollope Society. And the problem is not just
that the right is clever and wicked and better financed, or that
voters are dumb sheep and incorrigibly reactionary to boot, or
that we've hit a run of bad luck.

So just maybe we've made some mistakes. We have, and
they come down to this: the left has completely lost touch
with the regular needs of regular Americans. We've lost the
ability to talk to Americans collectively about the things that
concern them the most: their jobs, wages, and standard of
living; their quality of life (a dirty phrase to progressives); what
they're getting from the government in return for their tax
dollars; the life of their communities and the safety of their
neighborhoods; the education their children are receiving and
their kids' prospects in a world that America clearly no longer

bestrides in the way it did when they were young. To be sure, there are people and organizations within the left working diligently on nothing but those issues, particularly those relating to wages. But most voting Americans simply do not identify those things with the left. Because over the years, especially in the last few years, the left has come to be viewed by many people—and not just conservatives, not just angry white men, but many potential allies—as pursuing narrow agendas that don't speak either to their basic needs in day-to-day life or to any larger vision for the society as a whole. As the scholar and organizer Joel Rogers has put it:

> US progressives today are organizationally and ideologically fragmented. And so they are weak . . . Weakness confirms their fragmentation, and thus further weakness, by inspiring a narrow and defensive politics, particularist in the extreme and lacking popular appeal . . . [The progressive community] does not even aim at such appeal. It does not mount broad programs of social moment, much less aggressively compete for power based on them. It seeks not to rule, but only to be tolerated, as a hodgepodge of essentially single-issue groups possessed of more grievances than ideas. For some, the resulting isolation from "the people" confirms illusions of saintliness. Its most immediate and obvious effect, however, is to guarantee political irrelevance.

"Possessed of more grievances than ideas." What honest assessment can disagree with that? The various components of today's left make appeals, usually with very limited aims, for this group or that; rare, though, is the attempt to speak to people as any collectivity beyond the narrowest demographic. And in speaking to people as members of groups—and only as members of groups—we've lost the ability to talk to the whole. Programs are designed, and agendas set, to benefit African Americans or women or gays and lesbians or the disabled. Their concerns must be heard and action taken, because the society that existed before we were able to talk about the particular hurdles any of those groups face is one that none of us wants to go back to. But the ways in which those agendas have been pursued have obscured the sense (which ought to be a conviction) that there exist needs and goals that the great mass of people share—needs and goals that are unifying and that transcend those categories.

And so voters see the left talking to this or that "community," but they get no hint that we acknowledge the existence of a group called "citizens" or "Americans"—or even, unbelievably given the left's historical roots, of a group called "workers" (in a political lexicon in which any tiny collection of aggrieved persons counts as a "community," the phrase "workers' community" has somehow never caught fire). Indeed, there is open contempt in left circles for these designations. I suppose most lefties greet the word worker with some residual toleration, although once in a while, if you express concern for workers, you are challenged: what about people on welfare? (I've actually had this conversation, in real life.) Besides, the argument goes, most of the working class, i.e., the white working class, votes conservative. To use the word citizens is to exclude illegal aliens, and is thus xenophobic and probably racist. How one then keeps faith with the notion—and this is terribly old-fashioned of me, I guess—that it is citizens who run, or who should run, the democracy, is a puzzle. Americans, of course, is the filthiest word of them all—it's nothing more than a code word for straight white men, preferably suburban and Southern or Western, and perhaps their wives, provided they mostly stay home like they're supposed to and vote GOP with hubby . . . like they're supposed to.

This kind of thinking has led to a brand of paranoia, or at the least, a sullen, smug, and joyless defensiveness in which many people on the left have fashioned themselves into a sort of police force for all manner of language, tropes, and behavior. When that point is reached, everyone becomes the enemy. So if you dare to speak about problems in the federal welfare program and how those problems might be corrected, you're a racist. If you assert that abortion is fraught with complication and nuance, even if you basically support abortion rights—indeed, if you even use the word "abortion," since "choice" has become the favored term, no doubt on the basis of some poll showing that people react to it more benignly— you are to be monitored. Such inflexible postures leave the left defending, in the name of fighting racism or "attacks from the right," an indefensible status quo: who, for example, really believes that the welfare system is just fine as it is, or that the only problem is that benefit levels aren't high enough? Of course it's true that many people talking about welfare reform *are* making thinly disguised racial appeals; but why must that fact translate into the suspicion that anyone who raises a reasonable question is up to the same thing? That sort of reflexive stance puts the left in a box from which there is no escape. We can refuse to think about redesigning welfare or immigration policy or affirmative action; meanwhile, we know very well who *is* thinking about redesigning them. So when the laws are rewritten, it's the right's handiwork. The left has taken itself out of the conversation.

I saw this up close during New York City's mayoral campaign of 1993, when Rudolph Giuliani invoked one of the despised phrases—quality of life. The general progressive response was, Quality of whose life?, meaning that when Giuliani used the phrase, he was not expressing concern about, say, the quality of the lives of homeless families. True, he wasn't, and he deserved to be called on it. Also true that his use as a symbolic target of the "squeegee men" who hang out at Manhattan bridge and tunnel approaches with dirty rags and force their "services" on motorists had next to nothing to do with most New Yorkers' very real problems. But underneath his less honorable presumptions, he was talking about something real. And it's real, of course, for New Yorkers of a wide range of colors and ethnicities and sexual orientations and income levels—indeed, more real for poor black and Latino people than for upper-class whites, fewer of whom need to rely on the subways, public hospitals, police, etc. The actual quality of people's lives—the cleanliness of streets and parks, the state of repair of mass transit and infrastructure—was a genuine concern in New York City. Giuliani at least offered voters a response to these problems; the left offered gestural labeling. This reached its nadir when some progressives started calling Giuliani a fascist. He's a bit of an ogre, with an undeniable authoritarian streak and a moderate-to-conservative ideological bent, but I've lived in New York City during his entire tenure and can testify that he has not attempted to ban opposition political parties or arrogate to himself broad emergency powers. (The worst sin in using the word, of course, is against the victims of real fascism.) The progressives' man, David Dinkins, lost, partly because he was such a captive of this sort of nonsense and partly because he was unwilling to write budgets that relieved middle-class and poor people instead of Chase Manhattan and the bond raters.

It's not hard to see the self-marginalizing effects of all this. How many people—black, white, Latino, straight, gay, whatever—can possibly live up to all the demands this left would make on them? I would imagine that to the decreasing number of people who even listen to us at all, we sound like a tiresome, hectoring old mother-in-law (is that, pardon the pun, relativist?). If that were all this might be funny, but the situation is worse than that. The categories in which the left currently thinks are simplistic and, ultimately, dishonest. They mute the realities of life as people live it, which are much more complex; a human being, as the French philosopher Alain Finkielkraut asserts, is "more than a cultural phenomenon."

A wheelchair-bound black lesbian, to take a person with four aggrieved identities, is also, let us presume, a voter, a worker, a churchgoer, a commuter, a purchaser of goods, a homeowner, a neighbor, a daughter, perhaps a mother. She also identifies regionally, as, let's say, a Philadelphian, a Pennsylvanian. On the basis of which identity will she participate as a citizen? It's impossible to say; it will vary from issue to issue. A comprehensive politics must address all those identities. The wheelchair-bound black lesbian, in addition to being female, black, lesbian, and disabled, is part of a vast, polyglot multitude, no different from many millions of American women and, in some cases, men. The left has been dogged about addressing her identity as female, black, lesbian, and disabled, far less so about addressing the others. It's quite true that the right's specialty is to deny her any accommodations on the basis of the first four, and thus those identities are necessarily a battleground. But somehow the left also manages to wrap her in a banner, stuff her in a uniform, until she is no longer a person (with, as we have seen, complicated and multifaceted needs) but a symbol, an essential expression of some -ness or another.

This kind of facile categorizing also means that no member of any one of the left's defined groups has any obligations to those beyond the group: you needn't seek outsiders' cooperation or hear their opinions, because they're somehow inauthentic. Not only are they inauthentic, but they're probably oppressors, particularly if they're white or male, intent on fooling you into further submission. What this means for the notion of a common culture, even a common working-class culture, is and has been disastrous. What it means for integration is disastrous.

So we have now a left that is best described as tribal, and we're engaged in what essentially has been reduced to a battle of interest-group tribalism. And it's a battle the right will always win, for three reasons. First, it is a brand of politics that is in fact inherently reactionary: solidarity based on race or ethnicity or any other such category always produces war, factionalism, fundamentalism. This is as true in America as it is in Bosnia, as it was in South Africa, as it has been in thousands of other places. Second, the numbers are on the right's side. Like it or not, there are more straight white people in this country than any other group. There are more suburbanites than any other group. There are, still, more people who think of themselves as comfortably middle-class than there are members of any other self-identified group. Writing all those people off, as the left has been, is the surest recipe for continued defeat—for the illusion of saintliness—that exists. Third, the left has only really succeeded a few times in this country's history and when it has, it's done so by expanding its ambit to include those who don't usually identify with it: by showing people outside the oppressed group how their interest lay in seeing members of that group lifted from oppression, or by gaining enough of a consensus in the society that a particular goal the left espoused had a real connection to the common good.

Martin Luther King, Jr., most notably and admirably accomplished the former. He found, in the critic Stanley Crouch's phrase, "the intersection of mutual identification" where whites who weren't directly affected by segregation could see the depth of the tragedy for those who were affected. The union movement in its various phases did the latter. The Triangle Shirtwaist fire and other episodes from the early part of the century demonstrated to the broader public that corrective reforms were needed. Later, in the postwar period, the unions' increases in membership, as Joel Rogers notes, "redistributed income toward their members, thereby helped stablize mass markets for consumer durables, and thereby inspired investment, which increased productivity, which lowered the real costs of consumer goods for everyone." Students opposing the Vietnam War managed to show millions of Americans

who had never doubted their leaders' foreign policy imperatives why those leaders were wrong, so much so that both
major presidential candidates of 1968 had to campaign on
their plans to get America out (but not enough so that the
winner of that contest ever completely did). Today, the gay
and lesbian rights movement has had some success along
these lines; that strain of gay activism that has been able to
show straight America that "we're just like you" has succeeded
in convincing at least some Americans of the simple, unam-
biguous truth of that statement, although of course, that line
of argument is often attacked as accommodationist by other
activists. In each instance, those pressing the case of the in-
jured found a way to talk to the uninjured. They weren't just
submitting grievances; they had ideas, and the ideas all had to
do with establishing a universal bond of some sort across no-
tionally distinct lines—worker to petit bourgeois, black to
white, gay to straight—showing both sides how they could
benefit from the alliance.

These are the points where the left can win. Particularist,
interest-group politics—politics where we don't show potential
allies how they benefit from being on our side—is a sure loser. It
will never do the left any good, for example, to remonstrate
against angry white men; it's the right that needs that phrase to
stay in the headlines, because as long as it's there in the papers,
it stays alive as a concept the right can exploit. This is not to say
angry white men don't exist. But what's the use in carrying on
about them? What the left needs to do is to transcend these
categories and turn the tables on this sort of talk entirely. We
can and should defend multiculturalism, but as Barbara Ehrenreich instructs, "let's remember always that at its intellectual
and moral core, the left isn't multi-anything . . . the left has to
be an attempt to find, in the rich diversity of the human world,
some point of moral unity that brings us all together." Finding
that point will let us rediscover notions like community, citi-

zenship, and Americanism and define them for people on *our* terms; we have to reclaim these words, and others, and stop acting as if every expression or idea that hints at collective action is just another stalking horse for oppression.

If it's so that we can't win anything playing tribal politics, then why is it that that's exactly the approach so many people on the left continue to take?

It turns out that there are some good reasons why this came to be. What has today degenerated into the too rigid interest-group schema described above began, really, after World War II, with what was then a necessary and overdue reexamination of traditional Western values emanating from the Enlightenment. To understand this well, one must adopt the mind-set, briefly, of 1945: exhaustion at two grotesque world wars and repulsion at fascism's depredations. This Western world that brought tolerance and progress and truth and universal rights—did it not also bring destruction, enslavement, genocide on a scale never before seen? Technological progress may have created the notion of happy consumers, bringing people (at least those in the advanced countries with disposable incomes) more goodies and prosperity than ever thought possible; yet it also created Zyklon B and atomic weapons and, in a far less horrid though still negative manifestation, the drudgery of the assembly line. Progress, the world finally understood, was a mixed bag indeed, and the Enlightenment legacy of liberal humanism, it turned out, had not been able to stop the rise of fascism. And so came the thesis, most famously advanced by Adorno and Horkheimer, that Enlightenment rationality was fated to turn on itself, that attempts to order nature and things would inevitably entail the ordering—that is, the subjugation—of people. The impulse devolved into the Holocaust and Stalin's purges and Hiroshima and Nagasaki at the worst of times; even at the best of times, it amounted to what Herbert Marcuse coolly called a "comfortable, smooth, reasonable, democratic unfreedom."

With all this came new attention to the West's relationship to what had only just been recognized as the Third World. Colonialism and imperialism were also the unavoidable by-products of the universalist ethos. Further, it was believed that whereas the Europeans had won their universal rights by throwing off certain vestiges of culture, history, and tradition (e.g., monarchy, feudalism, theocracy), Third World countries could win their rights away from the colonizers only by dint of assserting their own culture, history, and tradition—which the Western powers had sought to suffocate, divide, or destroy. So the 1950s and early 1960s saw the left embracing not just Third World independence movements, but wholesale repudiation of the principles on which the First World had been built. Frantz Fanon made the argument:

> National claims, it is here and there stated, are a phase that humanity has left behind. It is the day of great concerted actions, and retarded nationalists ought in consequence to set their mistakes aright. We however consider that the mistake, which may have very serious consequences, lies in wishing to skip the national period. If culture is the expression of national consciousness, I will not hesitate to affirm that in the case with which we are dealing it is the national consciousness which is the most elaborate form of culture.

What person committed to liberation and decolonization could argue with that in 1963? Algeria had won its independence in a brutal war against France, the new nations of Africa and Latin America were serving as a chessboard for American and Soviet competition, and, of course, what was in store for the Vietnamese could scarcely at that point be imagined. White European culture had a lot of blood on its hands and a lot of explaining to do.

These intellectual pursuits wore down articles of faith in Western countries that had been accepted for decades, and, arguably, nowhere more so than in the United States—which, after all, was the only Western country to have established itself on the graves of indigenous people and on the enslavement of millions of Africans. The battles waged by the Old Left over the proletariat-as-agent question, over the Soviet Union, over the Rosenbergs and McCarthyism didn't matter much anymore to the younger generation. Further, this generation's emphasis was much more on domestic politics, on problems in America, than on debates about international socialism that, after the Twenty-sixth Party Congress especially, had lost much of their heft. The New Left, the roots of which can be traced especially to a group of students and academics at the University of Wisconsin in the late 1950s, but which first gained notoriety in Berkeley during the Free Speech Movement, followed the leadership of thinkers like C. Wright Mills and bit into the liberal establishment with a healthy vengeance: "As the architects and custodians of the warfare state, the liberals have been the primary generators of the anti-democratic trends in American society," wrote the editors of *Studies on the Left*, the UW-based journal of the New Left, in 1962 (the year of the Port Huron Statement). So the New Left leaders were changing the game drastically, being far more engaged in activist politics and, it's fair to say, operating less on reasoned intellect and more on instinct. A quote from Jerry Rubin from back then sums up the differences between the Old and New Left fairly well (and note the last word): "Who the hell knows from communism? We never lived through Stalin. We read about it, but it doesn't effect us emotionally."

As the '60s moved along, the New Left became associated with several developments: the civil rights movement, interracial in practice and strictly integrationist in principle until about 1966; opposition to the war in Vietnam, which enabled tendencies that were by then splintering to continue working together; and finally, following from the rejection of Western culture that Fanon described, the flowering of an antiestablishment culture. But that counterculture was really several countercultures, united around certain broad points but in fact quite disparate. By about 1968, the schisms were too marked to ignore. The early leaders of the New Left—all white men, who had more or less considered it their birthright in 1962 to step to the front of the room and lead the discussion—turned out to be just about as piggish as the liberals they denounced when it came to allowing women and minorities to have power. It wasn't just a question of internal democracy but of external emphasis on what were only just beginning to be called "women's issues" or, as it was sometimes put back then, "issues of interest to the Negro." In 1969, the Stonewall uprising began the gay liberation movement. A little later came the environmental movement; still later, others. Within each of these there quickly developed factions upon factions, riven by disagreements over this or that question. It's not difficult to see what happens to an idea like "universal values" in such an atmosphere. As Todd Gitlin has put it: "If there seemed in the late 1960s to be one big movement, it was largely because there was one big war. But the divisions of race and then gender and sexual orientation proved far too deep to be overcome by any rhetoric of unification. The initiative and energy went into proliferation—feminist, gay, ethnic, environmentalist."

These movements coincided with—were made possible by—the appearance of a philosophy that explicitly countered Enlightenment-based modernism's emphasis on absolutes, universal values, reason, progress, and science (and its fuzzy utopianism). Postmodernism, as the author David Harvey put it, "swims, even wallows, in the fragmentary and the chaotic currents of change as if that is all there is." So postmodernism argued against what are called meta-narratives, e.g., Marxian or Freudian analyses that could explain everything, and against universal standards, and for particular explanations, accidental explanations, sometimes no explanations at all. It encouraged fragmentation and difference, and postmodern ex-egeses of language and of power relationships demonstrated the ways in which our supposed democracies in fact trapped and encaged us, or most of us, or some of us more than others. The appeal to emerging political movements made up of people who had previously been shunted off to the sidelines (or worse, beaten and jailed) is obvious. The thinkers who advanced this "'68 Philosophy"—Michel Foucault, Jacques Derrida, Jean-Francois Lyotard, and so forth—were mostly French; on our own shores, writes Paul Berman, American radicals took a bit of this and a bit of that,

> and *voila*: the great new melange, '68 Philosophy in its American mutation. Its name is, or ought to be, "race/class/gender-ism," since "race, class, and gender" is the phrase that dominates its analysis.

As Berman goes on to note, "class" is thrown in mostly as a sop, a nod toward the old-timers and sentimentalists who still insisted on a vague vote of confidence in class-based and materialist analyses (even as many postmodernists were attacking them). This is not to say that one finds no class awareness in '68-style politics, but it is to say that there are ways in which race/gender (and sexual orientation) politics and class politics are profoundly incompatible.

The rest is, to modify the old cliché, recent history. A closer look at where the left stands today will provide much of the substance of Chapter One; suffice it to say for now that the purpose of sketching out the above history—and admittedly, any such brief rendering of complex ideas and movements tends inevitably toward caricature; I've merely tried to hit on the broadly relevant points—is to show two things. First, that circumstances have worked out the way they have for a reason. The current period of the American left's history may be depressing in the extreme in terms of its influence on public affairs, but it arose from conditions that made the pursuit of particularist agendas not only necessary, which sounds a touch grudging, but right and, indeed, courageous in many cases. How many gay people who came out after Stonewall were vilified and cast out of their homes and neighborhoods, or were beaten? How many black Americans were murdered or beaten in the civil rights era? How many countless Third World people died in their wars of independence? Not idle questions.

Second, however, history affords us the perspective to see just how wrong things have gone—how notions that were useful and exciting and new in 1968 have stiffened and have, in the hands of lesser intellects than Foucault and his contemporaries, turned into tepid parodies of themselves. We can see now why the right has full purchase on words like "citizen," or on notions like "standards," in school curricula, in art, or whatever. Equality of opportunity? For whom? What's "equality"? What's "opportunity"? (Some even ask, What's "of"?) We can now understand why the left makes no strenuous effort to organize beyond narrowly defined groups, and why attempts to connect the particular concerns of groups to the broader collective good are halfhearted at best: the notion that there even *is* a collective good is regarded with deep suspicion. And if that's your view, why do mass politics? If society is incorrigibly racist, sexist, and homophobic, if extant power structures cannot be changed because they'll simply re-create themselves, what's the point of doing anything, of leaving one's room?

Some critics have even questioned whether these new categories of politics are really so new, and—the crucial question—really progressive at all. Thus the argument that the identity-based left is merely our present-day version of anti-Enlightenment German Romanticism and, without trying to be melodramatic or unfair, we all know where *that* wound up. Indeed, the postmodernists and poststructuralists saw Heidegger, a brilliant philosopher but an enrolled member of the National Socialist Party, as their forebear, more than Marx or even someone like Gramsci. And there is, after all, a rough historical parallel between the first romanticists and the postmodernists: the romanticists rose up in early-nineteenth-century Germany in reaction to Enlightenment thought and its devaluation of explicitly national cultures; a few decades on, their ideas had rigidified in some instances into social Darwinism and the anti-Semitism one saw in the Dreyfus case. Similarly, it's true today that, in many cases, race/genderism has given way to a too rigid essentialism. What started as Black Power has in some cases ossified into racial (and sometimes blatantly racist) nationalism and, in more benign forms, reflexive and uncreative thinking about possible new approaches to racial problems. Much criticism of straight white men (not angry white men, just straight white men, even if they have generally "good" politics) within identity groups comes down to, You can't possibly understand because you're not . . . . And so on.

One can see also, in this context, how some of the poles that were previously reliable have reversed themselves. If all words, ideas, and concepts are fungible, if nothing has durability, then things can potentially be twisted to mean anything. Or, as some old-school Marxists will still tell you, give things enough time and they'll eventually become their opposite. So it is now mainly the left that attacks free speech; it is the left, in some cases, that now opposes integration and racial mixing; further, there have been blatant examples on the left of anti-Semitism, fewer than emanate from the nativist right, no doubt, but more than can be dismissed as an aberration. All in all, tendencies that I suspect many people reading their morning paper would find it hard enough to wedge under the rubric "progressive." Indeed, on the evidence, one might assert not that '68-style politics is inherently progressive, but that it has withered into something that is inflexible and intolerant.

It is for this reason, in addition to but above all others, that left and right don't even mean anymore what they have historically meant. What is one to make of a world in which to be on the left is to support, as many black nationalists do, racially separate schooling, a condition of reaction we thought we'd overcome 40 years ago? The end of the Cold War accelerated the confusion, not because many American or Western European leftists held out any hope for the East, but because the simple existence of socialism, benighted in the Soviet form as it was, served as a critique of and check on capitalism, forcing capitalist powers into certain accommodations. In the United States, this meant that relative domestic harmony and sharing of the bounty were of some importance, lest too much discord weaken the common will to fight the evil empire. Once those patinas were less vital to maintain, the gloves came off; enter the radical right, whose ascendance is probably thus tied to the fact that capitalism no longer has an enemy to fight. Today, the radical rightists and the militia people, their anti-Semitism and loonier ideas notwithstanding, are positioned athwart the state in ways that do resemble some aspects of '60s radicalism: their demands for local autonomy and their view of the federated state as illegitimate. In a world like this, it's no wonder that it's sometimes hard to know where to stand. Even the journalist Alexander Cockburn, certainly no wallflower on matters ideological, has written that he's "just about ready . . . to junk the whole left/right taxonomy as an impediment to thought and action."

Impediment it is, but more to the point, a sideshow; because who profits when left and right are locked in cultural battle over epidermis and genitalia? For the people who own the country, this battle is a pure godsend. Nothing could be better, from the point of view of fluid capital, than to have the white and black working classes at each other's throats, fighting over their respective share of the crumbs instead of uniting to increase the share for all. Not a week goes by that the business pages don't carry more news of downsizing and restructuring by some corporation, with the attendant job losses and the related social costs. This is where community values begin to break down, and without a strong, unified movement of the working and middle classes, nothing exists to check it.

This is where we are; not, by any means, a happy place. And we have to face up to the fact that we got here, in no small part, through our own doing. The particularism and intolerance, the miserly spirit, the self-righteousness and sniping, the plain lack of great and unifying ideas—and ideals—have brought a once great movement to its knees. And the left is paying the price at every level of politics: ideologically, organizationally, electorally, you name it.

This book is an attempt to remold and revive the left—or at least to spark a conversation that should have started years ago about what we've done wrong and why, and where we should go from here. Many people on the left, especially given the defensiveness that pervades what exists of the movement these days, will see only the attack and none of the loyalty. Likewise, readers outside the circle will be tempted to ignore the loyalty and regard the attack with glee. To be sure, an attack it is; but an attack born of despair, not disgust, and an attack whose goal is not to bury the movement but to resurrect it.

Why? Because working people in this country need a movement that will put their interests and livelihoods first. Neither conservatism nor liberalism is doing that adequately. Conservatism, as the public should discover eventually, is at bottom for the rich, or at least for those members of the middle class who don't need much help, and numerous polls have shown that people are not as conservative as the House Republicans wish them to be. Liberalism, on the other hand, has failed to answer most working people's needs. Domestic liberalism worked fairly well as long as people's wages were going up; but that stopped in 1973, and liberalism—and the Democratic Party, now almost as deeply in hock to corporate benefactors as the Republican Party—has not fashioned a strong response. Furthermore, liberalism did get too bloated; it has fallen into the inevitable pattern whereby, lacking new ideas and approaches, the only thing to do is to become ever more precise and picayune about the old ones. Regulatory agencies write rules that are sometimes silly, like determining how many inches above the floor a workplace handrail should be. The correct measure is 42 inches, and woe to those whose rails are 39 or 46. One congressman told me about a constituent who lived near the water (and thus in a wetland) whose deck extended out a few feet too far; the state environmental officer (young, by-the-book) was ready to drag the luckless stiff (working-class, minding his own business) into court. The constituent, the congressman said, understood well that the Clean Water Act had tidied up the bay to the point where he could fish in it again, but his sense of goodwill toward the liberal state was evaporating over the deck issue. This is a mere anecdote, but there must be thousands like it. For every person who responds to perceived government snoopiness by going out and joining a militia, how many more must there be who continue to abide by the law but respond by stewing in their living rooms, or voting Republican? It's a far vaster army, and *they* sure aren't liberals.

The two major parties and their ideologies just aren't working well for enough people. Today, barely one in five American adults carries out the duty of the franchise with regularity, and even these voters, or at least those who respond to a ceaseless parade of polls, are constantly expressing deep anxieties. And so one senses that the old categories are in the process of exploding, and that we're on the cusp of immense political change. The mood is sour and foul, which has been often observed, but it is also confused, contradictory, fragile. Like the butterfly effect, by which a butterfly flapping its wings in Beijing theoretically can affect the weather in New York, so does any combination of farflung circumstances appear capable of making American politics shoot off in any given direction. What butterfly, what slight, inscrutable motion, will set it spinning?

My wish is for the left to set events in motion. To do so, it will have to crawl from its current wreckage and figure out how to become a movement of the people again. The history is certainly there. It's always been the left that has fought for better lives for powerless people, that has pushed the notions of social justice and personal freedom constantly forward— against, it should go without saying, intense and often violent opposition from the powerful. And the left did not accomplish these things by scrutinizing textbooks for hints of various -isms and phobias, but by changing the actual conditions of people's lives. When women garment workers faced deplorable conditions, it was not the right that helped unionize them and win them protections. Coal miners, steel workers, automobile workers—the right saw their injuries, their permanent disabilities, and their deaths as just so much spoilage factor against the bottom line; it was the left that made their lives better. When no one else was bothering about black Americans' rights and earning power, white leftists did, going back to the abolitionists, and later to Communist Party efforts to organize sharecroppers in the 1930s, and finally to the freedom marchers of the 1960s. This list could go on, but the point is that these were victories for points of view that were thought outlandish in their day but are now accepted by almost everyone as proper, as the correct advance of history.

Those victories were possible in part because the left was fluid and flexible, able to change its priorities from generation

to generation. What was crucial for John Reed and his contemporaries was not necessarily so important for the Old Left
that followed. Years on, the New Left was quite different altogether from the Old Left. Each of those twentieth-century
versions of the left hit about 15 to 20 years after the preceed-
ing one; but now, 25 to 30 years after the New Left was at its
apogee, what has followed it? We've got no cohesive movement, nothing that we can call really new—just worn out
simulacra of the New Left movements, their agents either en-
sconced in the academy or out there tilling the fields but with
far less success and energy.

This book will argue for a new movement, one that recognizes and advances the causes that emerged from the New Left
but that also understands that those causes have to be woven
into a greater whole; that they can't be the sum of our politics,
but rather must be part of a broader politics that is based on the
conviction that the nation is more than a collection of tribes.
A movement that synthesizes the particular into the universal,
instead of merely celebrating the proliferation of more and
more particulars. That restakes some claim to Enlightenment
thought and argues not that democracy and progress and truth
are nasty and antiquated ideas that should be defenestrated,
but that they remain ideals that haven't been fully realized. Finally, a movement that can talk again to those outside it and
make them identify with those within (and, by the by, a movement that's fun and mischievous and irreverent, because the
right seems to be having all the fun these days).

And, although the focus of this book is America, it's important to realize the ways in which a revitalized American
progressive movement can, literally, change the world. The
United States alone, simply because its power and wealth are
still so vast, can set the direction for the rest of the advanced
world to follow. A revivified progressive coalition here will
perforce create its counterparts in Europe. An America that

rises above its own particularisms and ethnic rivalries might be able to posit itself as an example for others, in Bosnia, in Macedonia, in Russia, in the Middle East and, with some credibility, lead a Western coalition that lays down principles that factions there must adhere to. And for the Third World, especially for the people making six dollars a day weaving those designer garments, an America devoted once again to working people will surely bear fruit.

In 1967, Martin Luther King, Jr., asked, Will it be chaos or community? His concern, to be sure, was for a movement that integrated, that pulled together the disparate and the far-flung; some will say the world has changed too much since King's day, that chaos has ineluctably imposed itself, and that the kind of community he spoke about is impossible now. The world *has* changed, but not that much. The chance is still here, but time is even more of the essence now than it was when King wrote:

> In this unfolding conundrum of life and history there is such a thing as being too late. Procrastination is still the thief of time. Life often leaves us standing bare, naked and dejected with a lost opportunity . . . We may cry out desperately for time to pause in her passage, but time is deaf to every plea and rushes on. Over the bleached bones and jumbled residues of numerous civilizations are written the pathetic words: "Too late."

That could be our epitaph, too, the way the left has been going. Certainly if the left doesn't change its thinking, and quickly, it *will* be too late. But the words that will mark our gravestones have yet to be written. It's time to take a hard look at the shape we're in, do something about it, and ensure that the inscription is a kind one.

Chapter 1

A HANDFUL OF SMOKE

What Is the Left?

E very year in New York City, on the first weekend of April, the Borough of Manhattan Community College is the site of the Socialist Scholars' Conference, put on by the Democratic Socialists of America. Readers who might be scared off, or turned off, by the word "socialist" should worry not; there's no screaming about the imminence of revolution, and spirits are typically at their most aroused when the bagel and coffee line opens. Nevertheless, it is, or used to be, a reasonably engaging affair, even in the dour years of Reagan and Bush; publishers set up tables and offer books at discount (sometimes; capitalism has its place, even there) and panels run over the two-day period in the classrooms upstairs. As the name suggests, it's geared toward academics, but the attendees also include journalists, activists, a few Democratic politicians, and a smattering of people who fall into none of those categories but who are in some way committed to the cause. There are, of course, the expected "stars" of the left, like Cornel West, and sometimes unexpected stars, like porn actress Nina Hartley, a self-described socialist who used to show up from time to time for the obligatory panel on pornography.

"Obligatory," increasingly, became the operative word. Sometime in the early 1990s, in fact, I and most of the people I know who used to attend regularly just quit going because it got to be like seeing the same movie over and over again, and not such a great movie to begin with. There were some very smart people on dozens of panels covering an amazing variety of topics; but somehow the overall effect was deeply perfunctory. Someone reasonably up to date on the literature had only to look at the list of speakers on any given panel to know exactly what ground would be covered. You could be sure no challenging or provocative new ideas or arguments would be launched, and you left after the second day with the sneaking suspicion that you had just fulfilled your role in a ritual in precisely the same way Kiwanis or Rotarians do at their annual meetings: attendees spend two days patting themselves on the back for being like-minded (and right-minded) and having their ideas ratified, then it's back to their respective hutches until next year, when the same thing will happen all over again.

Over time, it occurred to me, the conference and its numbing array of panels had become emblematic of the condition of the contemporary left in general, demonstrating how difficult it had become even to speak of something called "the left." There is not really a single left today but a collection of several small lefts, divided among and even within themselves, sometimes agreeing on things, sometimes not. There is the traditional, labor-based left, but it has shrunk in size and influence, partly because the labor movement isn't what it used to be and partly because it is in some ways out of touch with the newer movements built around race, gender, and sexual orientation. There is the black left, which upon inspection is divided into several competing camps, from Afrocentric to nationalist to assimilationist, with a thousand points in between. There is the feminist left, similarly riven; so is the gay and lesbian left. We have an environmental left, an animal rights left; a left that seeks to connect social change with religious values, and a left that seeks to crush all vestiges of religion and the family. There is a cultural left for which "transgressive" art and alternative lifestyles are central to the fight against authority and bourgeois mores and for personal autonomy and pleasure. On foreign policy matters, there exist sharp disagreements about America's role in the post-Cold War world, with some arguing, for example, in favor of Bill Clinton's intervention in Haiti, based on their belief that the restoration of Jean-Bertrand Aristide was in keeping with democratic values (my view), and others arguing that the United States, through its agents in the Pentagon, will ultimately act only in the interests of the imperium (a position, I confess, not to be taken lightly). The question of Bosnia has deeply divided leftists along similar lines: I once interviewed Todd Gitlin for an article on the subject, and he told of how he and a few friends who had "always agreed on everything" began discussing Bosnia one evening and, to their collective astonishment, "every conceivable position was represented." Some of these kinds of disputes were on amusing display in 1991 at marches against the Persian Gulf war, where sentiments ranged from the studied and somewhat overwrought Support the Troops, Oppose the War position to the out-and-out hard line taken by some of the more revolutionary tendencies, Defend Iraq! Defeat U.S. Imperialism!

Given all this, it's worth asking the most basic of questions: what is meant today by the left? What does it include and not include? Many people these days shy away from the word itself, assuming that it may scare off potential allies or carry too much baggage. The preferred term of art over the last several years has become the softer and somewhat saccharine "progressive"—this denotes a person or a movement that is to the left of standard liberalism but is not quite leftist and certainly not socialist. In 1989, I covered a City Council election on Manhattan's Upper West Side—what better place?—in which eight candidates seeking an open seat turned cartwheels trying to out-progressive one another, each investing the word with greater brio than the last during candidate forums. The U.S. Congress has a Progressive Caucus consisting of those members of the House of Representatives who lean furthest toward the left, such as Vermont's Bernie Sanders, a socialist, New Yorkers Major Owens and Jerrold Nadler, California's Maxine Waters, and a handful of others. Their agenda is fairly left-wing, but no congressional agglomeration, one can be sure, would ever call itself the Leftist Caucus. There is some irony in the widespread use of the word, because the Progressive Movement of the early twentieth century was rooted in a broad, class-based populism, and today's left is anything but populist.

Are liberals part of the left? To listen to the right wing tell it, the two are indistinguishable; from the point of view of Rush Limbaugh or any number of other commentators, Bill and Hillary Clinton are radical leftists. True, there are certain cross-fertilizations between left and liberal that to some extent support the Limbaughesque contention, and these—specifically, the emergence since the 1970s of a liberal-left identity-based coalition—will be covered in the next chapter. But for most people within the left, the Clintons aren't part of the movement by a long shot. Wasn't Bill Clinton one of the founders of the Democratic Leadership Council, which sought to move the party toward the center and away from the discredited liberal policies of the past? Clinton had a chance to establish a bit of a leftish credential during the 1992 campaign when the question of his draft status arose. He could have said straight out that he had opposed the Vietnam War and could not morally justify participating in it. Instead, of course, he made every effort to distance himself from opposition to Vietnam, supposedly to retain his appeal to the nebulous and misconstrued "center" he is ever so eager to please. Of course, this center has been suspicious of him anyway, not least because he's such a waffler. Instead, taking an actual stand on Vietnam might have earned him some respect from the people who saw the folly of that war (and there are many) and helped erase the waffler image, which has been stuck to him like quick-drying cement.

The gulf between left and liberal is not just about the Clintons, of course. There are vast historical arguments between radicalism and liberalism. There's no need to go into those here in any great detail, and some of them will be discussed in the following chapter. And in any event, time has chopped away at some of the reasons for those differences. No one today can talk seriously about dismantling capitalism, for example, which was the main project of the left in America in the first decades of its existence (say, the 1870s to the 1930s). Similarly, no one today can talk seriously about the possibility of world socialism: capitalism has shown a resiliency and fluidity that old leftists did not anticipate, and it looks like it's here to stay. Besides, the Soviet Union and its satellites were police states, as is Cuba, and one can harbor serious reservations about disparities of wealth and related problems under capitalism while still bidding good riddance to those corrupt systems. Further, with the Cold War over, traditional left-wing opposition to U.S. geopolitical aims, which set it quite apart from liberalism and its willingness to support the basic imperatives of the Cold War state, is no longer relevant or reliable—hence the arguments within the left over Haiti and Bosnia, and even the support, in some leftist quarters, of the Persian Gulf war.

One can see the old categories crumbling by examining not just the left but the right, where those who want to see the

United States maintain its hegemony in world affairs support arming the Bosnians while others—the isolationists—insist that it's not America's fight. Probably the sharpest example of the blurring of the old lines was evidenced by the North American Free Trade Agreement debate, during which Pat Buchanan, Ross Perot, and the American labor movement stood shoulder to shoulder in basic agreement over the "great sucking sound" that would be heard—indeed, that is being heard—as formerly American jobs move to Mexico's *maquiladora* zone and other points south and east. Indeed, Buchanan's presidential candidacy, if one puts aside the jingoism, is explicitly left-populist. That is took a Republican presidential campaign to open discussion of America's class fissures tells us much about both the priorities of the Democratic Party and the weaknesses of the left.

So we return to the original question: what is the left? The left today exists in just a handful of places: first and foremost, in the remnants of the 1960s civil rights movement; second, and relatedly, in the movements that learned their organizing techniques from the civil rights movement but that represent other identities and groups, specifically the women's movement, the gay and lesbian rights movement, the Latino movement, and the disability rights movement; third, on a few campuses and in small segments of the academy, where the hubbub over "radical orthodoxy" far outstrips any influence radicals have in point of fact; fourth, among some but by no means all segments of organized labor; and finally, among some environmentalists. I suppose we should include an "other" category made up, say, of various intellectuals without a campus affiliation (e.g., journalists) and of activists in areas like housing or legal defense. These activists do admirable work, but their number is negligible.

It is, in other words, primarily a left composed of "communities," as the phrase goes, based on race, ethnicity, gender, and sexual orientation. The labor movement still has some sway, particularly when it comes to political endorsements, but by and large its seat is in the back of the bus. The vanguard, without question, is the identity movements; people are identified and described as representatives of this or that community, and these are the categories in which people reflexively think.

And what percentage of the general population does this left comprise? It's really impossible to say; certainly no opinion polls ever bother to ask respondents if they consider themselves leftist or radical. But we can make an educated guess. Look first within what remains of the civil rights movement. Black Americans constitute about 13 percent of the whole population; how many of that 13 percent would consider themselves left? Right off the top, take away the 50 or so percent of that 13 percent who rarely bother with politics or voting at all. Of the voting half, assuming they behave like the population as a whole, perhaps a fifth or a quarter do anything of a political nature beyond casting a vote, like making a political donation, volunteering time to a candidate or cause, reading lots of political books, writing letters to the editor or to elected officials, what have you. We're already down under 2 percent, and some of those are conservative (not many, but a growing number, alas) and most are probably liberal with reservations—they vote Democrat for the obvious historical reasons but they may oppose abortion or gay rights or support the death penalty. From here, one can only guess; but with numbers so infinitesimally small, what's the difference whether it amounts to .18 or .32? Of course, the civil rights movement included, and includes, whites and people of other races in supporting roles; whether that number today is 10,000 or 100,000, it's still tiny relative to the general population. We might be talking, all in all, about a half-million people.

This is not to say that far larger numbers can't be rallied to certain causes that pop up from time to time—the Jesse Jackson presidential campaigns, which were pretty left-wing for 1980s America, being the most obvious example. Unfortunately, the causes about which black Americans most often show political solidarity are not necessarily left or progressive causes but racial ones. Certainly the two need not be mutually exclusive, the Rodney King beating being a prime example. But on other matters, white leftists tend to follow the lead of race activists, so cases like those of Tawana Brawley and Ben Chavis, it's sad to say, were black/left causes in their day. That two such controversies—one surrounding a teenager caught in a web of lies presumably spun by two lawyers (now disbarred) and the other involving sexual harassment allegations against the head of one of the country's most respected civic organizations—should become "causes" is pathetic, but that's how things go these days. But they become so when white leftists, whether out of guilt or fear, patronize black opinion, as many did during the Brawley affair. The Million Man March was certainly an instance of racial solidarity, both to the good and, because of Louis Farrakhan's prominence, to the bad. Where it fit on the ideological spectrum is somewhat more complicated; blacks expressing a sense of collective power and will is undoubtedly a progressive act, but Farrakhan's leadership of such a movement means that it has the potential to be deeply reactionary.

The women's movement is probably somewhat larger, first of all because women make up just more than half the population as opposed to 13 percent. But radical feminism, the movement that began in about 1967 and forced so many changes in American society, scarcely exists anymore as a movement. The National Organization for Women, then considered by more radical feminists a milquetoasty liberal outfit, must stand today (given the rightward shift of the political spectrum) as the leading liberal-left feminist group. It claims 250,000 members nationwide. Of course it must be noted that NOW's membership is dwarfed by that of the two leading conservative women's groups. Phyllis Schlafly's Eagle Forum and Beverly LaHaye's Concerned Women of America boast nearly 700,000 members between them. It is true that most American women— 71 percent, according to one 1995 poll—identify themselves as "feminists" when feminist is defined as someone who supports "political, economic, and social equality for women." But that's as standard a definition of feminism as you can get, and women answering yes to that definition will include many who support those things in general but are uncomfortable with, or oppose, other aspects of the agenda of NOW and other groups such as the Feminist Majority Foundation, which commissioned the poll. The National Abortion Rights Action League and the National Women's Political Caucus are two membership-based groups that make endorsements at election time and help women candidates. But unless it's your view that electing women is an inherently progressive act, it's hard to call these groups progressive. NARAL, especially, is so in thrall to its single issue that it will endorse candidates, especially incumbents, who support abortion but oppose every other mildly liberal cause known to exist. In any event, the question arises again, as it did with respect to blacks, as to how many self-identified feminist women have left politics across the board on a broad range of issues. Again, polls don't measure these things, but whatever the final number is, it can't be terribly large—certainly much closer to the 250,000 who pay their dues to NOW (we presume they pay, anyway) than the 71 percent who will tell a pollster they're feminists. Recently, feminist action groups made a brief comeback; WAC, the Women's Action Coalition, and WHAM, Women's Health Action Mobilization, both of which started in New York City, attracted small but influential followings for a while and staged public actions or "zaps" around the city on topics like rape and domestic violence and AIDS awareness. Neither group lasted very long, though. The

Guerilla Girls, a group of women artists in New York who, through posters and performances, raise issues of discrimination in the arts and in politics, have showed more staying power, small though they are.

The gay and lesbian movement? Kinsey's famous 10 percent has fallen into serious disrepute in recent years, with some estimates of gays and lesbians in the whole population going as low as 1 percent, others putting the number at 4 or 5 percent. Whatever the case, again, the subsegment that is politically active on the left is tiny. Some gay activist groups have been highly visible in recent years: ACT UP, an organization best known for its deeply misguided assaults on New York's St. Patrick's Cathedral, but which has in fact done good work in other venues; Queer Nation, a kind of ACT UP offshoot; and the Lesbian Avengers, a lesbian action group with chapters in several cities (the Lesbian Avengers and Guerilla Girls, much as I may disagree with their heavily identity-based politics, at least have a sense of humor).

Latinos make up about 9 percent of the American population, and the number on the left probably works out roughly the same as for black Americans—except that as a group Latinos are more conservative. One finds the expected empowerment groups in cities where Latinos are concentrated, but again, whether these groups are single-issue oriented or genuinely progressive across the board on a range of matters varies widely. The disability rights movement consists of some relatively small percentage of the 20 million disabled people in America, and in any event is relatively particular in its interests.

In the academy, left-wing teachers probably number at most a few thousand. By and large they are people who were students in the 1960s and thus were part of the New Left in its heyday; in this sense, the New Left, a student-based movement from the start, never really left campus. Saying this is of course not the same thing as saying that leftists dominate the academy, which is a ridiculous claim, with the possible exception of a very few small private colleges and a handful of urban public ones. Despite the rhetoric of some on the right, which helps them sell lots of books and command fine lecture fees, most universities have a handful of radicals here and there in English and humanities departments, in the women's studies and African studies departments that emerged after the '60s, and scattered thinly about a few other departments. Meanwhile, in business, marketing, mathematics, chemistry, biology, forestry, engineering, and other departments—which is to say, among the vast majority of faculty and students— politics scarcely even enters into things. Of course there is student activism, always an important part of radical activity and not to be overlooked—student activism was crucial, for example, in the South Africa divestiture movement. But for numerical purposes, most fit into one of the other, identity-centered categories.

The next group, the labor movement, is obviously much smaller than it was 20 years ago. Roughly 13 percent of the American work force is unionized, or about 17 million workers. But of course, there are unions whose racism and conservatism is appalling (police unions, drivers unions, some construction and industry unions), and there are unions that are mobbed up to their eyeballs and have thus lost the right to be thought of as unions at all. Further, the line between radicalism and unionism is no longer anything approaching a straight and strong one. In the 1994 elections, 40 percent of union members voted Republican. In the end, not all that many unions are even vaguely leftish these days: some traditional union members like mine workers, autoworkers, machinists, and meatpackers; some government employees; some health and hospital workers; some communications workers; some oil and chemical workers; a few others. The AFL-CIO's election last year of John Sweeney as its new president, in its first openly contested electoral fight, was supposed to revitalize American labor; we shall see what we shall see. Let's be kind and say the labor left numbers 4 million, all the while being aware that, unless American life changes in ways utterly unforeseeable today, that number will continue to shrivel.

The environmental movement, broadly speaking, can claim some 15 million adherents in terms of membership in the major environmental organizations. But environmentalism is, in the main, not a radical movement (strain of a tendentious zealotry among many environmentalists is undeniable, but it's not the same thing as radicalism). Major environmental organizations such as National Resources Defense Council and the Sierra Club are very mainstream groups—richly financed with highly effective and well-connected lobbying operations. Greenpeace, in rank and file terms, is somewhere to the left of Sierra or NRDC. There *are* some genuinely radical environmental groups, mostly in the western states, that have fought off-shore oil drilling and the logging industry. In cities, there are the radical urbanists, who draw attention to urban environmental crises like toxic dump sites in neighborhoods. There are also many small environmental community-based groups: these are citizens' organizations that fight, say, an incinerator in their town. They do good work, but rarely are they linked to other left groups.

The "other" category would consist mainly of people who get paid for their activism, like legal services attorneys and those who work in nonprofit housing and poverty organizations and the like. The totals can't be more than, again, a few thousand. So finally, what are we talking about here? Two percent of the overall population? Four or five? Whatever the case, it's a minuscule figure. Ah, you say, but wasn't it always this way; wasn't the left always tiny relative to the population at large, gaining its influence not so much from sheer numbers as from the prominent position of a few intellectuals and leaders? The answer is no, it was not always this way. In the 1930s, organized labor was as close to being on an equal footing with big business in this country as it will likely ever be, and it was far more militant then than it is now, even among its staunchest anti-Communist members. And, of course, it commanded far more attention. When United Mine Workers President John L. Lewis gave a speech, all three networks carried it live over the radio; only Franklin Roosevelt commanded an equal audience. Today's labor leaders are doing well to make tape delay on C-SPAN. In the 1960s, when the civil rights movement was at its peak, it can fairly be said that millions of Americans participated in that revolution. Whether they marched or sent money or did volunteer work or simply expressed support at their local community group or house of worship, many millions of people contributed to the dismantling of American statutory apartheid. The nation's soul was bound up in that movement. Today, the civil rights movement is a relatively small and elite group comprising mostly academics and lawyers—it manages to bring people out in numbers for the cameras from time to time, but most of its work is done in boardrooms and courtrooms. The broad base upon which left social movements always depended has dried up considerably over the past 20 or so years.

With tiny constituencies come tiny ideas. Very little has emerged from today's left except agendas pursued mainly on the basis of group membership and mainly through the law and the courts, rather than through the broad-based moral suasion of the public. And court-imposed solutions that lack broad public support are ultimately very weak foundations for social change. These methods have led down a path that narrows and narrows as ever more fanciful and arcane theories are advanced in order to achieve aims, and anyone who doesn't support those theories is branded as an enemy of progress. Hence the left's self-marginalization.

An excellent example of this is the hate speech debate. Here we find in convergence every lamentable tendency the left falls prey to: the emphasis on group identity and the outright denial of either individual or universal identity (and also of universal values, such as freedom of speech); the forging ahead through the legal byways without attempting to establish anything approaching popular consensus; and the reliance on finely wrought legalistic arguments that will do nothing at all in practical terms to change the world—except, possibly, to harden and strengthen the opposition. The end result is that the First Amendment is placed at risk, with little hope that the types of speech these proposed codes seek to punish will actually ebb and the ironic prospect that such laws, if enacted, will be used against the very "oppressed groups" they're intended to protect.

The hate speech debate is a relatively new one. After decades of cross burnings and other acts of hatred often went unpunished, a consensus finally developed in America that expressions of hatred against minorities would not be tolerated. Yet of course incidents continued to occur, and liberalism seemed, to a small group of radical legal scholars, incapable of punishing the perpetrators or changing their behavior. So by about the late 1980s, a new movement was born to outlaw racist, sexist, homophobic, and other types of injurious speech, and thus protect members of historically oppressed groups from its effects. In fact, this idea was not really so new at all. Michael McConnell, a University of Chicago law professor, has written that the first piece of hate speech legislation in America was promulgated not in the 1980s, or even in the 1960s, or at any point in U.S. history at all, but back in 1649. This was colonial Maryland's Toleration Act, meant to protect the "free exercise" of religion. Lord Baltimore, Maryland's founder, was Catholic, and he hoped to make Maryland a Catholic haven— a place that would be sensitive to the Catholic community's needs and desires, we might say today. Thus was a ten-shilling fine imposed on those who called others "by such opprobrious terms as, Heretic, Schismatic, Idolator, Puritan, Independent, Presbyterian, Popish priest, Jesuit, Papist, Lutheran, Calvinist, Anabaptist, Brownist, Antinomian, Barrowist, Roundhead, and Separatist." Today only the terminology has changed. Instead of religious denominations or sobriquets, insert terms of insult based on race, gender, and sexual orientation and you have a 1990s hate speech law.

There were similar such laws among the various colonies— amazingly, South Carolina's, written in part by John Locke, outlawed denigration of Jews—and later among the states. It is in fact one such group libel law, upheld by the Supreme Court in *Beauharnais v. Illinois* (1952), that hate speech theorists cite as providing a possible precedent on which their work can build. The law upheld by *Beauharnais* proscribed expression that "portrays depravity, criminality, unchastity or lack of virtue in a class of citizens of any race, color, creed, or religion." Critical legal theory, whose chief practitioners include Mari Matsuda, Richard Delgado, and Charles Lawrence III, cites this case and several others as evidence that such protections have existed in the past and can exist again without an abridgement of civil liberties. It places primacy on the wounding power of words, and even equates words with acts: "Oppressive language does more than represent violence," the author Toni Morrison has said. "It is violence." It also attacks the current, widely accepted interpretation of the First Amendment as being content-neutral—which means that laws should not favor a single idea over others—and argues in favor of an approach that is content-specific—meaning that the law must brand certain types of hate-filled speech as unacceptable based on what we know about this country's history and power relationships. Matsuda developed three criteria that define racist speech: it must convey a message of racial inferiority; it must be aimed at a historically oppressed group; and it must be "persecutory, hateful, and degrading" (Matsuda links this last to the old notion of "fighting words," which the Supreme Court has ruled are not protected).

On the surface, it seems hard to disagree with this; who, after all, is in favor of speech that is "persecutory, hateful, and degrading"? But as Henry Louis Gates, Jr., wrote in an essay in *The New Republic*, making distinctions like the ones Matsuda suggests is, in real life, nearly impossible to do. Racist speech against, say, Jews and Asians, is not likely to convey a message of inferiority but rather of sinister superiority. And what, Gates asks, is an historically oppressed group? "It is just a matter of time," he writes, "before a group of black women in Chicago is arraigned for calling a policeman a 'dumb Polak.' Evidence that Poles are a historically oppressed group in Chicago will be in plentiful supply; the policeman's grandmother will offer poignant firsthand testimony to that." Indeed, this "reverse prosecution" effect seems to have held sway in jurisdictions where speech codes have been introduced. When the University of Michigan had a speech code in place—a code, remember, designed to protect minorities—nearly two dozen blacks were charged with racist speech, and not a single white. In Florida, a black man was prosecuted for calling a white cop a "cracker." The first hate speech case to get to the Supreme Court featured a white plaintiff and a black defendant. And so on. This too, it turns out, is not so new; the only recorded prosecution under Lord Baltimore's act was of a Catholic.

Finally, what is degrading to one person is not necessarily degrading to another, which raises the question of whether the prohibition will include just obvious epithets or more refined statements that someone, somewhere, still considers injurious.

Where, we might ask, is the NAACP's class action suit against Charles Murray, the estate of his late co-author of *The Bell Curve*, Richard Hernnstein, and this publishing house? Are not the Cleveland Indians and the Atlanta Braves lawsuits just waiting to happen? When will the first suit be filed by a woman who resents being called attractive rather than intelligent, by a white man who would like to be called "homeboy" but is instead called "whitey," or by the parent of a bespectacled child over another child's playground invocation of "four eyes"? Every person becomes his or her own censor. One needn't look too hard to see there is potentially no end in sight, with the effect that society fragments further and further into its smallest constituent elements.

Reverse enforcement and unenforceability, though, are just the beginning of the problems. It must be asked: what will such laws really accomplish? Does anyone seriously believe that tough laws against hate speech will make it disappear? We have tough laws against murder, rape, and drug dealing in this country, laws that have been getting tougher every year; and for most of those years, until very recently, the crime rate in America increased dramatically (recent crime reductions are primarily attributable to different policing strategies, not tough sentencing or the death penalty). Of course, this is precisely what will happen with hate crimes—not only those relating to speech, but to acts as well. Bias crimes legislation, which punishes acts of violence motivated by bigotry, is perhaps more defensible from a First Amendment point of view but is equally flawed in presuming that behavior can be corrected through punitive reinforcement. If a white man goes to jail for killing a black man and the sentence is lengthened because he said the word nigger while doing it, how will that change the white man's heart except to harden it? Under the federal hate crimes bill (thankfully not passed), he need not even say it. If evidence of prior bigotry is produced at trial, even if that bigotry was not "exposed" during committal of the crime, years can be tacked onto the sentence. Is this really what the left wants? The irony of the left, which has argued for years that many offenders can be rehabilitated, shouting, "Lock 'em up and throw away the key," is scarcely believable. It is not by accident, by the way, that the only group the left wants to lock away is straight white men, at whom these codes are really aimed and who are, by the hate speech theorists' definition, oppressors and not oppressed, no matter where and under what conditions they live, no matter how much money they make, whether they buy and sell buildings or sweep those buildings' floors. And, of course, bias crimes legislation can be used against minorities too, as in the case of the black youths who killed a white person after they saw the film *Mississippi Burning*.

And what of the First Amendment? Forget the absolutist arguments that the right now conveniently wields; the right has usually stood against absolute freedom of speech in America's history, a truth to which any mildly left-of-center person of prominence who was alive in the 1950s can testify vividly. But there is the argument, undeniable in my view, that expansion of rights and expansion of speech go hand in hand, that the former cannot proceed without the latter, and certainly never in a climate that seeks curtailment of speech. Yet this is what the hate speech left proposes. They will apparently risk what is arguably their greatest and most fundamental right as Americans so that they may procure a right—as I've shown, a right that can be used against them—as members of a self-identified group. "For the first time in American history," writes Christopher Hitchens, "those who call for an extension of rights are also calling for an abridgement of speech." He continues:

> The Constitution, which is elastic to infinitude about potential expansion of rights . . . is also adamant about free speech and assembly and about the wrongness of an established faith. Thus

every great battle for the extension of liberty on this continent has had, in the last resort of the Constitution, the law on its side. And most if not all such contests have necessitated a parallel battle for the principle of free speech and assembly.

So the civil rights movement was also a movement in favor of freedom of assembly. Any effort to form a union begins with picketing, leafletting, printing a newsletter. If you think suffragism in the 1910s or feminism in the 1960s could have flourished as they did rooted in this kind of thinking, check out the vast array of newsletters that various feminist groups of both eras published (and note, in those of the latter period anyway, the abundance of robust name-calling, undoubtedly "insensitive," that filled their pages). And yet, here we have today's left, arguing that speech properly regulated will be somehow "empowering."

Finally, the equating of speech with action, an idea that the critical legal theorists lifted from antipornography warrior Catherine MacKinnon, blurs the line between the rhetoric of empowerment and the real conditions of people's lives. The idea that speech and action are the same thing is absurd, as is the idea that placing a cordon of disapprobation around a certain type of speech can have any impact whatsoever on the world's material conditions. Gates writes:

> The problem may be that the continuing economic and material inequality between black America and white America, and the continuing immiseration of large segments of black America, cannot be treated simply through better racial attitudes . . . [T]he political economy of race and poverty can no longer be reduced to a mirror of what whites think of blacks . . . In some ways the intellectuals have not caught up to this changing reality. Generals are not the only ones who are prone to fight the last war. Rather than responding to the grim new situation with new and subtler modes of socioeconomic analysis,

we have finessed the gap between rhetoric and reality by forging new and subtler definitions of "racism."

Jonathan Rauch, writing in *Harper's Magazine*, described this tendency as "the new anti-pluralism," which he labeled "purism" because "its major tenet is that society cannot be just until the last traces of invidious prejudice have been swept away." Naturally this is impossible, and one suspects that the purists know it's impossible but motor ahead anyway, safe in the knowledge that as long as bigotry exists, they'll always have something to complain about and will always be able to land the next foundation grant. And their complaint is a powerful tool these days. I'm aware that, as a result of the foregoing paragraphs, I will be called a racist by some, or at least insensitive; but knowing this, and having been called lots of things over years of scribbling out my political opinions anyway, I'm more or less prepared. Most people's hides are thinner, though. Consequently, people who disagree with speech codes or racially drawn congressional districts or the affirmative action status quo, even if they're on the left and possess enough credentials to rest on, will usually keep their mouths zipped forever rather than risk being called a racist. And so are enemies made of people who raise legitimate concerns.

I have dwelled on hate speech because, as I said previously, it perfectly encapsulates the worst elements of radical activity these days. It may not seem as though it's a major issue but in fact it is, at least potentially: municipalities and college campuses are still busy trying to enact hate speech laws. Someday, somewhere, a major case will work its way through the court system and, if the purists have their way, the First Amendment will be back where it was, say, during World War I, when Woodrow Wilson and his rampaging postmaster general, Albert Burleson, revoked the mailing permits of many publications that ran antiinterventionist articles. You hardly need me to tell

you which side of the political spectrum those publications
were on—the same side that will inevitably suffer from the very
speech proscriptions it advocates today. We tend also to forget
that the First Amendment's place is a tenuous one. It was only
in 1931 that free speech protections became the absolute ones
we know today, so much precedent exists for speech protections to be rolled back. And even though the current Supreme
Court struck down such a law from Minneapolis, I'd prefer not
furnishing this court with any temptation to revisit those days.
And meanwhile, the miserable poverty of many black people
and other Americans, the second-class status of many women
and gay people will continue, words or no words.

The left couldn't possibly serve the right a better platter.
Indeed, the right knows very well what's been handed to it,
and conservative campus organizations oppose speech codes
at colleges and enjoy the sympathy of a majority of onlookers.
An issue that was ours for years is now theirs.

And of course, hate speech codes, along with bias crimes
laws, though originally conceived of within the academic
left, have now become the province of liberals as well. Thus,
university administrators and Democrats in Congress and
elsewhere prattle on in well-rehearsed fashion about putting
bigots away. Mario Cuomo, as governor of New York, carried
on about his hate crimes bill for years, strumming his violin,
going for the sympathy of the multicultural crowd by blaming
the Republican-controlled State Senate for preventing it from
becoming law. The fact that so many Democratic liberals (and
indeed, some Republican conservatives) have taken up this
particular cause tells us that it wasn't very radical or challenging to the status quo to begin with. It also provides a good
introduction to a longer discussion of the relationship between
the left and the Democratic Party.

Chapter 2

MARRIAGE OF INCONVENIENCE

The Left and the Democrats

Every four years, as another depressing presidential campaign sags toward its conclusion, people on the left ask one another the same mournful question: So are you voting for him? Him, of course, is the Democratic presidential candidate, and though who he is may change with each election and the particular issues may shift around the edges, the basic arguments reappear every fourth November as reliably as morning frost. Mondale/Dukakis/Clinton isn't on the left; M/D/C is a sellout, a hellspawn of the establishment, the hand-picked and bought-off candidate of the elites, his pockets stuffed with the dirty money of the usual corporate interests. Those who think there's any hope of real social change in electing M/D/C are fooling themselves. True, Reagan/Bush/Bush is worse, but is that what it's come to, the mere selection of—to use the phrase that gets such a workout on the left—the lesser of two evils?

Words rush back and forth in torrents as to whether a vote for a mainstream Democrat is a respectable one. *There's no difference between the two major parties.* Oh yes, there *are* some differences; just look at civil rights and abortion, for example. *A Democratic administration will give the left "maneuvering room" for its activism, and at least some left-wing voices will have access to power.* No, a Democratic administration will in fact choke off activism, because once the right is thrown out, people will get lazy and expect their liberal friends to take care of things. *You're actually considering voting Republican? That's unconscionable!* But I see little difference between the two candidates and anyway, a Republican vote is a strategic vote; the worse, the better, says the dialectician in me. *Well, won't the Democrats at least rein in defense spending?* Are you kidding? The Democrats will spend even more on weapons programs, since they have to bend over backwards to prove to the hawks they're not "soft on defense." *OK, well, what about the judicial system? There is the Supreme Court to think about.* Sure enough, it's the high court line that is often the clinching parry in these jousting matches, which any person on the left can recount in full comic detail.

These questions were more hotly debated in 1992 than in any other recent election. Compounding the usual ponderings about whether a Democrat could be expected to move in a progressive direction was Bill Clinton's explicit promise to move the Democratic Party away from the liberal edge, to pinpoint the vital center and make liberalism less . . . well, liberal. He had demonstrated this intention as a governor by taking stands against labor in his right-to-work state and by trying to position himself as a pioneer on welfare reform. He demonstrated it remorselessly as a candidate when he flew back to Arkansas from the New Hampshire hustings to oversee the execution of a man with the mind of a three-year-old, a man who left his dessert uneaten in his cell when they took him to his death because he didn't understand that he would not be returning. For these and other reasons, people on the left were especially distrustful of Clinton, far more so than of Michael Dukakis or the old liberal dinosaur Mondale.

And yet Clinton, everyone knew, stood a better chance of being elected than any Democrat since Carter. Not because of his centrism necessarily, but because he was young, handsome, a compelling candidate as these things are judged, and a Southerner; because the economy was suffering and George Bush was such a bleating goat through most of the campaign; and most of all, because Ross Perot, apparently out to stick it to Bush, made it possible for someone to win with less than a majority. So even though he was more distasteful, he was far more likely to carry the day than other recent Democratic nominees. The prospect of voting for someone who might actually win, after which we'd be partly responsible for putting him in office, obviously intensified the vexations of leftist voters.

In the end, though, it wasn't much of a dilemma at all. The bleak prospect of four more years of Bush pushed all but the hardiest or most doctrinaire into the yes camp. The month of the election, *The Progressive* ran a symposium entitled, "What, Me Vote?" in which two dozen figures associated with the magazine were asked the big question. Only four of the 24— Samuel H. Day, Jr., Nat Hentoff, Herbert Hill, and Colman McCarthy—said they'd shop elsewhere, a proportion that more or less confirmed what I had found in casual conversations. If anything was surprising about *The Progressive*'s respondents it was the degree of enthusiasm expressed for the man by Molly Ivins, Ronnie Dugger, Susan Douglas, and several others. My newspaper at the time, *The Village Voice*, had whacked Clinton mercilessly throughout the campaign yet endorsed him with enthusiasm in the end. There were lots of fights and friendships were threatened, and though the situation seemed dramatic at the time, it was in fact not so different from previous presidential elections. Look up issues of any left-wing journal or magazine during other presidential election seasons and see for yourself. "Why Vote for Johnson?" *Dissent* asked in 1964. The somewhat overwrought answer was that "voting for Johnson may be a political act, but it will not change the relationship of forces in this country, which are heavily weighted towards reaction and neofascism." Those exact words could have been said of Clinton by someone on the left, and in fact probably were somewhere.

But the presidential question is merely the most intensely focused expression of a debate the left has engaged in for years: is the Democratic Party friend or foe? The answer has varied over the years. Obviously, the left has had no use, and vice versa, for the various moderate and conservative Democratic factions down the decades—the Dixiecrats, the boll weevils, the Democratic Leadership Council centrists. But liberals have probably constituted the most stable bloc within the party in the postwar period, at least until very recently, and certainly liberals and leftists have often shared the same general goals—equality and justice, world peace, a social system ensuring certain comforts for all. Disputes have centered around what's needed to achieve them—optimistic liberals say reform, skeptical leftists say revolt. But there have also been fierce disagreements: on U.S. policies during the Cold War, which most liberals supported and the left opposed, on communism and anti-communism, and on the meaning of loyalty and patriotism. So the answer to the question of whether the Democratic Party is the left's friend or foe, as the sketched history that follows will try to describe, has varied from period to period.

Increasingly since the 1970s, the answer is friend. I'll examine this in more detail below, but basically what's happened is that the Democratic Party of the early 1970s, led by a wing that was more liberal than usual, made an effort to bring under its tent people who'd previously been excluded from party procedures. These were representatives of the various disadvantaged groups that were constituencies of the New Left. Simultaneously, the party took on these groups' agendas as platform items and policy goals—usually not too difficult to do, because the goals were narrow and not really challenging to either the party's or the country's power structure and class relationships, and because doing so was a way to secure these groups' votes. Bringing in the excluded and supporting issues like abortion rights are laudable acts in themselves, but, at the same moment, something rather less salutary happened. The inclusion of previously disfranchised groups ended up necessitating the exclusion of longtime Democratic constituencies, leading to the alienation from the liberal left of the white working class, both Southern Anglo-Saxon and Northern ethnic, that continues to this day.

To compound matters, this development has taken place at the same time that the two-party system has fallen gravely, and deservedly, into disrepute. Most political analysis doesn't entertain the possibility of opposite tendencies occurring at the same time, but that's how things are in the world sometimes. So it was that, in the very years that the Democratic Party came to accept the agenda of the New Left groups—that it became the party of abortion rights and, increasingly, gay rights—it also became the party of both corporate America and official Washington—financed more and more by huge multinational corporations, in hock to wealthy lobbies, and part of a system that, for most regular working people, had become inaccessible and corrupt. An identity-based left has hitched its wagon, in other words, to a political party that in the same era has become increasingly elitist. This is why it so resonates with working-class people when Dan Quayle or William Bennett speaks of a "left-liberal elite."

In the old days, when there was a large, mass-membership, class-based left genuinely to be reckoned with in America, there was no debate whatever on the point of solidarity with Democrats: the Democratic Party was a capitalist party, and that was that. There were factions within the left, of course, some more revolutionary than others, but radicalism was potent then, and it showed its potency at the polls. Eugene Debs ran for president five times as the standard-bearer of the Socialist Party; twice, in 1912 and 1920, he polled nearly one million votes (the 1920 election was especially impressive, considering that he was in jail at the time). Woodrow Wilson had few admirers on the left, particularly after bringing the United States into World War I; the red scares after the war, which Democrats as well as Republicans encouraged, and the rise of the Ku Klux Klan, which Southern Democrats abetted, kept the distance firm. Running for president in 1924 under the Progressive banner, Robert LaFollette, Sr., polled nearly five million votes.

In the 1930s, things changed a bit. The election of Franklin Roosevelt and the interventionist economic course he was charting through the Depression made the relationship between the left and the Democrats more complicated. FDR did push through wage legislation and other bills protecting workers, and progressive independents were welcomed into his administration (Labor Secretary Frances Perkins and Interior Secretary Harold Ickes, for example). But the 1930s being the radical, volatile period that it was, there remained much left-wing opposition to Roosevelt. It never coalesced into anything that even remotely challenged his status—much like today, third-party efforts broke down and dissidents and critics mostly came around to the Democratic candidate at election time—but the left undoubtedly had far more impact on the debate in those days than it does today, and thus it had some success in pressuring Roosevelt to move the New Deal along more rapidly than he might have preferred.

Radicals fell into essentially two groups in the '30s. Most radical elected officials, like Minnesota Governor Floyd Olson ("Minnesota is a left-wing state!" he crowed in 1933), could be called native radicals—they were perhaps socialist in some way, but they had no taste for European radicalism and were utterly uninterested in the doctrinal arguments over the Soviet Union that occupied the thinkers of Old Left intellectuals in New York and that filled the pages of the *Partisan Review*. The native radicals were, in their own way, American exceptionalists—not jingoistic, but nevertheless certain that European nostrums could not work here. Their magazine was *Common Sense*, and their forebears were Paine and Jefferson rather than Marx and Lenin. To them, the New Deal was not going far enough fast enough, and they were constantly snapping at Roosevelt in much the same way that Jesse Jackson snaps at Clinton today, with the rather crucial difference that they had vastly larger constituencies. The second camp consisted of what might be called doctrinal radicals: party-affiliated Socialists and Communists. Their rejection of FDR was simple: Roosevelt was a capitalist or was trying to save capitalism, and thus was an impediment to the revolution (about which, needless to say, Socialists and Communists had very different ideas). Both parties ran their own presidential candidates—Norman Thomas for the Socialists and Earl Browder for the Communists. There were some commonalities between the natives and doctrinals. Thomas, in particular, was a popular figure among many radicals; running for president in 1932, he polled roughly as well as Debs had at his best, collecting 840,000 votes.

In the end, the native radicals really gave Roosevelt more trouble, to which he generally responded with a combination of rancor and charm sufficient to hold them at bay. In the 1934 off-year election, brothers Bob and Phil LaFollette ran as Progressives for governor and senator of Wisconsin, respectively, against Democrats. Both won. Their rhetoric, Phil's particularly, was quite radical: "We are not liberals! Liberalism is nothing but a sort of milk-and-water tolerance . . . I believe in fundamental and basic change." Roosevelt was friendly with Bob Jr. at first, but not for very long. In Louisiana, Huey Long, whom FDR disliked and feared, was putting forward his Share Our Wealth program, which was well to the left of the New Deal, although not terribly well thought out and darkened by Long's dictatorial tendencies. Long would have run against FDR in 1936 had he not been assassinated the year before in Baton Rouge (Long even wrote a book, *My First Days in the White House*, in which he allowed that it would be possible, in a Long administration, for FDR to head his old department and become Secretary of the Navy). Out in California, author and longtime socialist Upton Sinclair actually won the Democratic nomination for governor on the strength of his EPIC (End Poverty in California) platform; Roosevelt, after promising to support him against a right-wing Republican candidate and a vicious slander campaign cooked up chiefly by MGM mogul Louis B. Mayer, hung Sinclair out to dry. Frank Merriam, the Republican, won handily.

Some of these disputes continued during the war, although in the main, the country pulled together to beat back fascism. But immediately afterwards, a second and ultimately much worse red witch-hunt began to heat up, and Democrats and the left were at loggerheads again. Truman, the president who created the national security state and launched the nuclear age, took America into a Cold War that the left would always oppose (the left has made its share of errors over the years, but its principled opposition to overt and covert U.S. intervention abroad during the Cold War is something to be proud of). Domestically, Truman seized the railroads and the coal mines and sent to Capitol Hill some of the most antilabor legislation imaginable. Many of the old congressional radicals, who had been the bridge between the left and the Democrats, were tossed out of office in the '46 and '48 elections. The left tried to rise again with the 1948 presidential campaign of Henry Wallace under the Progressive banner. His admirable platform—disarmament and banning the bomb; internationalization of the Suez and other hot spots; a unified Irish homeland; indemnities for interned Japanese Americans; national health insurance; more public works; legislation to wipe out the poll tax and to raise women "to first class citizenship"— was something the Democratic Party of 1948 would never have tried. Wallace, not a Communist or a Socialist, was a radical, and he was red-baited to death, not just by leading conservatives like columnist Westbrook Pegler but by Truman himself ("He ought to go to the country he loves so well and help them against his own country if that's the way he feels" was a typical dig). Wallace's campaign also made some silly mistakes, and he finished well below early expectations with 1.15 million votes.

The 1950s, of course, were a dark hole. There was some radical activity, it's just that it couldn't amount to much. The journal *Dissent* was founded, chiefly by Irving Howe, who remarked about the situation that "when intellectuals can do nothing else, they start a magazine." McCarthyist hysteria ended up costing not only leftists but many liberals their livelihoods and positions in society. Some liberals abetted these witch-hunts by distancing themselves from the left and denouncing "communism," which in the stoked atmosphere of the day often ended up meaning anyone or anything the least bit pinkish. Liberal and ex-Communist intellectual Sidney

Hook attacked Communists and remarked that nothing in the Constitution or the Bill of Rights, not the First (or any) Amendment, guarantees any absolute rights (this line of argument should sound sadly familiar to readers of the previous chapter). Americans for Democratic Action, a liberal group, was vehemently anti-Communist, and the American Civil Liberties Union accepted only applicants who could swear that their love of liberty was "not qualified by adherence to Communist, Fascist, Ku Klux Klan or other totalitarian doctrine."

By the late '50s, when this madness abated, left and liberal entered a period that was at least less stressful. Arthur Schlesinger, Jr., writing in *The Progressive* in 1959, outlined a liberal platform he hoped many on the left would take up: equal rights for minorities; a revamped educational system; slum clearance and community revitalization; and so on. Responding from the left in *Dissent*, Emanuel Geltman suspected that Schlesinger was "whistling in the dark": the issues were the right ones, but the Democrats and their putative new president (whether Kennedy, Johnson, or whomever) would probably lack the will to carry the program out. Schlesinger and Geltman each turned out to be about half right: the Democratic Party made civil rights a key part of its platform and President Kennedy did take some steps, such as confronting Alabama Governor George Wallace, but he also did his best not to have to push the matter too much.

Meanwhile, of course, there was another set of Democrats. Senators James Eastland and John Stennis of Mississippi, Congressman Judge Smith of Virginia, and dozens of others like them in Congress and the statehouses were scarcely hospitable to anything remotely similar to what Schlesinger had suggested. But even as Martin Luther King, Jr., was leading the civil rights revolution and a Democratic president, Lyndon Johnson, was taking risks to codify it, an episode occurred that served to remind people on both sides that reforming the nation's laws might in fact be less fraught with dangers and difficulties than reforming the party's. When the Mississippi Freedom Democratic Party tried to gain recognition at the 1964 Democratic Convention, Democrats reacted in the expected fashion. Johnson, desperate to receive wild acclamation, tried to browbeat all into compromise; the racist Southerners scornfully went home without pledging loyalty to him; and liberals, worried that agitation would result in their man Hubert Humphrey being dumped from the ticket, failed to back the MFDP publicly. The compromise was flatly rejected by the MFDP—"We didn't come here for no two seats," goes Fannie Lou Hamer's famous quote—but approved by the floor. Johnson saved some face; Mississippi, in an adumbration of what was to come, voted for Goldwater; and the dissenters took seriously a pledge from the Democrats that party rules would be amended to prevent future discrimination in party affairs.

Next, Vietnam, and whatever goodwill Johnson had won from the left as a result of his civil rights and antipoverty programs vaporized. By this time, the American left, which throughout the 1950s had consisted primarily of New York intellectuals on the one hand and homespun, populist politicians from various parts of the country on the other, was first and foremost a student-led movement—white, primarily, but working in close alliance with black groups like the Student Nonviolent Coordinating Committee, the Black Panthers, and many others. This younger and angrier left needed little encouragement to take to the streets on behalf of civil rights or against the war. Then King was assassinated and then Bobby Kennedy, the chosen candidate (after Gene McCarthy fizzled) of many New Left leaders and, for all his unsavory past associations with Roy Cohn and the like, the last presidential contender we've had in America who stood a chance of bringing poor whites and blacks together. New Left leader Tom Hayden wept as he watched RFK's funeral, although—in a gesture perhaps symbolic of the continuing divide between liberal and left—he refused an invitation to ride on the train that carried RFK's body to Washington ("the people on the train . . . had not proven any interest in the grass-roots people who cared about Kennedy"). When the Democrats' convention in Chicago exploded in tear gas and mace, establishment liberals and the radical left shared nothing.

Yet it was at just this point that today's relationship between the two was forged. That same convulsive convention had mandated the creation of a commission—building on the promise made in 1964 to the MFDP—to open up party rules. Commencing work the following year, the McGovern-Fraser Commission, named for co-chairs George McGovern and Minnesota Congressman Donald Fraser, promulgated 18 new guidelines for state committees to follow in choosing delegates for future national conventions. Several rules were directed at making state primaries more important than deliberations in smoke-filled rooms. And crucially, guidelines A-1 and A-2 required representation in each state of women, young people, and minority groups "in reasonable relationship to their presence as a population in the state." This development was simultaneous with the left's evolution into its current incarnation as an amalgam of several identity-based lefts. The McGovern-Fraser rules were designed to accommodate these groups, and with the influx of these new faces into the delegate structure, it was no wonder that it was the South Dakotan whom they chose to nominate in 1972. And so McGovern's liberal-left coalition was born. Clearly, there were elements within the left—some substantial ones—that wanted nothing to do with McGovern or the Democratic Party and that saw participation in electoral contests between the two parties as a useless sellout. But it is fair to say that McGovern was the candidate of the New Left—its shot, as it were, at big-time electoral politics. Certainly the obverse was true: McGovern was far more a candidate of a movement than of a party, because all the party regulars knew, and this required utterly no prescience on their part, that Nixon would crush him.

That movement precipitated a showdown freighted with symbolism when McGovernite forces undertook to unseat the delegation of Chicago Mayor Richard J. Daley at the 1972 convention. The Cook County delegation numbered 59 and Daley, it should go without saying, had paid little heed to the new guidelines, A-1 and A-2 least of all. An alternate slate was selected but, as Theodore White wrote, "no one quite knew how." This slate comprised a large number of representatives of disadvantaged groups from Cook, well *out of* proportion to their number in the general population. A raucous fight ensued, after which the credentials committee voted the new slate in, 71 to 61.

In one respect it's difficult to say there was anything wrong with what the McGovern troops did. Daley was a bigot, and the matter might never have become the problem it did had he shown some degree of fairness in the selection of his delegates. So blame in the first instance rests squarely with him (and with all the other smaller Daleys around the country who did the same thing). That said, there is much truth to what columnist Mike Royko wrote in an open letter to one of the aldermen spearheading the anti-Daley move:

> I just don't see where your delegation is representative of Chicago's Democrats . . . [A]s I looked over the names of your delegates, I saw something peculiar . . . There's only one Italian there. Are you saying that only one out of every 59 votes cast in a Chicago election is cast by an Italian? And only three of your 59 have Polish names . . . Your reforms have disenfranchised Chicago's white ethnic Democrats, which is a strange reform.

This, of course, was the summer of 1972. But the direction of the liberal-left McGovern coalition was apparent well before then. Michael Novak, then a liberal Catholic writer, had picked up on the problem that March:

> McGovern is chiefly a spokesman of the national liberal culture. He voices the views of the educated class, highly mobile, traveled, its members more in touch (by journals, books, films) with each other than with local culture . . . There is too much moral superiority, arousing of guilt feelings, preachment. There is not enough feeling for and with people. . . .
>
> The white lower middle class, particularly in urban areas, is the key to the politics of the future . . . The enlightened are bigoted regarding the unenlightened: that is our major strategic problem. The enlightened mean well, they are capable of change, but they have a longstanding contempt for parochial, rough, direct, ordinary people.

At that point there was perhaps still time to change things, but nothing really did change. Andrew Kopkind, the late radical journalist and New Leftist who was certainly not one to apologize for his (or the left's) politics, nevertheless noted the phenomenon when he traveled to Illinois in 1977 and reported on the nascence of the New Right. "The New Left and its descendants," Kopkind wrote, "have been notoriously maladroit in reaching people whose background and behavior diverge from its young, white, cool, cosmopolitan styles and middle-class status." He described the wall that several working-class Catholic women ran into at an Illinois International Women's Year planning session when they declared to the session's leaders that, *although prochoice themselves*, they could scarcely go back to their neighborhoods "and organize other women on the basis of the purist platform" that the organizers had put forth.

Of course, none of this had happened in a vacuum. Back in 1963, GOP leaders made the calculation that their party could differentiate itself from the Democrats, and thereby substantially realign American politics, by opposing civil rights (there had been pro-civil rights planks in the previous two party plat-forms). A year later, when Goldwater carried five states in the Deep South, the vote-getting potential of this position was clear enough that by 1968 Richard Nixon and his aides were able to speak of a "Southern strategy." It was a straight-on strategy of inciting racial fear to win the white vote, especially the working-class white vote. It worked; Goldwater did mark-edly better among poor Southern whites than Nixon had in 1960, and by the time Nixon came back around in '68, the poor-white Southern vote was fast becoming solidly Republi-can at the presidential level, as was the white ethnic vote in the Northern cities. George Wallace's incipient campaign that year, strongly flavored with anti-Washington populism, drew votes away from Nixon in the South, but what was more im-portant was that Nixon and Wallace combined—the antilib-eral vote, in other words—garnered 57 percent at the polls. And insofar as the Wallace campaign affected liberals and the left, it served only to drive home another point: populism, once almost wholly identified with left-wing figures like the LaFollettes, Long, and Sinclair, was now firmly a right-wing phenomenon, and inexorably a racist one.

Given Nixon's and the Republicans' despicable stratagem, perhaps there was nothing McGovern's liberal-left coalition could have done to try to keep poor Southern whites and Northern white ethnics in the fold at a time when that coali-tion was giving people who had never been consulted a voice for the first time. Certainly, to accomplish that would have taken a style of rhetoric and a set of policies that no person to date has been able to concoct. But we'll never know, since no serious efforts to do it were ever made.

What we do know is that for the left, this defection of so many working and middle-class people, and the left's resulting increased identification with selected liberal elites, is easily the single greatest political tragedy of the last 25 years. An admirable, necessary, and quite overdue development—the inclusion of people who had been discriminated against up to that point—was dragged down by a damnable one. It was bad then, and it's simply worse now. This, at bottom, is what the 1994 elections were all about. The Republicans won the House of Representatives because they got enough angry white men—and working-class white women who, unlike better-off women, voted Republican in '94—jazzed up enough to vote. This is what was set in motion in 1972, and I would say that it reached its apotheosis in 1994, except that it is possible the wave has not yet peaked.

This also was the milieu in which Bill and Hillary Clinton came of age—they worked on the McGovern campaign, as did their Deputy Chief of Staff, Harold Ickes, Jr., and other Clintonites. And these, by and large, are the politics they picked up. Further, the left groups that were first influencing electoral politics then—civil rights groups, women's groups, environmental groups, and the gay and lesbian movement to a slightly lesser extent—are established organizations today—multimillion-dollar corporations, really—with limited memberships perhaps, but with a relatively sure path of ingress nevertheless into the newspaper columns and chat shows. In other words, both ambitious yuppie liberals like the Clintons and more ideologically committed people who are likewise members of the chattering class have arrived. They have power, and when they talk to each other they do so at a haughty remove from most regular people. Hillary Clinton may be a fine symbol for many American women, and it can't be doubted that the right has made her a target for many bad reasons. But when she says, as she during the famous Gennifer Flowers controversy, that she's not some little woman standing by her man like Tammy Wynette, or that she has better things to do in life than stay home and bake cookies, she belittles millions of American women who don't fit her conception, and that of the elite women who take out full-page ads in the major papers to defend her, of what a woman ought to do.

The moment of high comedy on this front came when Clinton was announcing his cabinet members. The naming of a cabinet today is one of those exercises in which success, from the liberal-left point of view, is judged in large part on the basis of melanin and estrogen—the more of each, the more "progressive" the cabinet is thought to be. Clinton was actually doing fairly well in this lukewarm regard; having started out with cursed old white men Warren Christopher, Robert Rubin, and Les Aspin, he named Laura D'Andrea Tyson to head the Council of Economic Advisers, Hazel O'Leary (who had the added benefit of being black) to steer Energy, and Betsy Moeller to head the EPA. But he backslid a bit with appointees like Dick Riley for Education, and so the cry went up: Where is Clinton's promised cabinet that "looks like America"? Liberals and leaders of the tribal left were, to use their favorite word, outraged. Clinton, seeing his leadership and his earliest key decisions challenged by many of the very people who'd been gushing over him, responded in kind. I am not a bean counter, he said. I'll pick the people who are best qualified, and if they "happen to be" (a phrase that makes a lot in overtime pay these days) black or Latino or female or gay, all the better.

Do I even need to point out the obvious, which is that he already had and duly continued to count beans in the most assiduous way possible? And so he announced that his choice for attorney general, the last crucial cabinet appointment not yet made, would be a woman, a gesture that tellingly put the lie to the whole whoever-happens-to-be-the-most-qualified business but at least revealed the process for what it is—a stage-managed exercise in feel-goodism that has more to do with assuaging the concerns of elite interest groups than anything else. For the left, "diversity"—expressed mainly in the appointing of people to leadership positions—is the symbol of a particular group's having arrived, having developed clout, having gained a seat at the table, or any of the other grating clichés that are invariably invoked on such occasions. For the liberal politician, diversity, by providing proof of "sensitivity," is as easy and cheap a way to buy off potential opponents and troublemakers as exists. As soon as I name a few women or people of color to high posts, the pol tells himself, they'll quit complaining and start praising me for my sensitivity. I may never have to do a single thing about real poverty or the bleak conditions of many black peoples' lives or the unequal pay for equal work that women receive as long as I keep those appointments coming. And I must remember to deny that an appointee has been selected because he's black, or because she's Latina, and to insist that the person was chosen because he or she is the best one available for the job.

Any politician can grasp this greasy stratagem in about two seconds. There is no other reason why Bill Clinton would denounce bean-counting on principle and then go on to count beans. And it's not just liberals who play this game, of course. Newt Gingrich, in the first two years of his term as Speaker of the House, named more women to leadership posts than Democrats did in 40 years. This has not made him a feminist, but it has made it quite difficult for those who place a high value on such symbolism to call his hand. Did anyone seriously believe that Clarence Thomas, a man who was generally believed to belong in the Supreme Court building primarily as a tourist, was the best possible choice for an open seat, as George Bush insisted? Of course no one believed it. Actually, the fact that some black leaders came out against Thomas—Jesse Jackson and Benjamin Hooks, who led the NAACP at the time—showed that there are limits to epidermal symbolism. But that limit is rarely reached.

Diversity, of course, does not extend to any considerations other than gender and skin color. Viewed in more scrutinizing light, Clinton's cabinet was in fact as lacking in diversity as any in history, for it included representatives of all the groups that have been running the country for years: a partner at a powerful Washington law firm; a Wall Street power broker; a couple of public officials from various states; retired politicians; a couple of academics at top universities; a few other corporate lawyers and executives. In other words, all people drawn from the ruling class, most either from large corporations or in the business of pleasing, representing, or somehow currying favor with same. The nominee for attorney general over whom fulsome tears were shed, Zoe Baird, was an attorney with Aetna Life & Casualty, one of the big five insurance companies that have for years been the nation's leading impediment to progressive health care reform, who was drawing a salary in late 1992 of $507,000 a year. When her nomination collapsed after the disclosure of her servant problem, Aetna welcomed her back to her old job in Connecticut, having recently bought her a new $650,000 home. It may be true, as feminists complained at the time, that Baird got tougher coverage than a man might in a similar situation; nevertheless, something tells me lots of people would be happy to suffer as she's suffering. Needless to say, far less attention was lavished on the poor servants than on Baird.

Genuine diversity is by no means a bad thing. It is absolutely crucial that black people and Latinos and gays and others be assimilated, and assimilate themselves, fully into society. This should include governmental appointments. There's nothing wrong with having, say, a black attorney general; in fact, there are very good historical reasons for it. But there are more important ways to help minority group members than through today's "rainbow" understanding of diversity, which is so devoid of ideology that a George Bush, a Newt

Gingrich, and even a Jesse Helms, who hired civil rights symbol James Meredith, can make use of it with aplomb. The inordinate emphasis placed on it amounts to nothing more than a series of arguments that few Americans have a genuine stake in or probably care much about.

Meanwhile, in the two decades that this coalition has asserted itself, the nation's capital has become a thieves' den, a nightmare of palm-greasing and wallet-stuffing predicated on a game that the public is by now well on to. Campaign "reforms" passed in 1974, in the wake of Watergate, were intended to make politicians and their money accountable to the public; they've amounted to nothing more than a form of legalized bribery, in part because the Congress—under Democratic control—still permitted all manner of so-called soft contributions so candidates could get around the rules. The reforms also served to ossify incumbents' protected status, because donors give steadily to incumbents of both parties and to challengers of neither—their ideology turns out to matter less than the business they have before particular committees. This, and the hyperexpansion of congressional staff, has created a permanent governing class in which both parties, their policy disputes aside, have really merged into one large Incumbent Party.

Lobbyists' influence also increased profoundly in this period. Washington lobbyists have always had power and access, but it wasn't until fairly recently that the two major parties worked up the insouciant nerve to invite corporations and their lobbyists to underwrite directly their conferences and gatherings. When congressional Democrats went to the posh, expensive Greenbrier resort in West Virginia in 1989, the $250,000 weekend was almost completely paid for by lobbyists, such as the man who had worked for the Senate Finance Committee and now lobbied for financial institutions and the woman who was a General Motors executive. The

name of the latter was Debbie Dingell, and she happens also
to be the wife of John Dingell, who at the time chaired the
powerful Energy and Commerce Committee, which handled
legislation of interest to his wife's employer. At a resort where
lodging and amenities can run a normal guest several hundred
dollars a day, members of Congress paid $500 each—not out
of their private resources, but out of their campaign funds. It
may seem like a bad joke to observe that right after this conference that Democrats resolved that members of the House
should receive a 51 percent pay raise, but it's true.

Horror stories about legal corruption and influence-ped-
dling are legion; I need not go on. And the left can't be blamed
for this, of course; indeed, the left press is diligent about expos-
ing these clammy scenes, and many hard-working people on
the left collect their meager paychecks lobbying in the public
interest against these corporations, while many others have
made campaign and lobbying reform, to sadly little avail, their
life's work. Jerry Brown was a favorite among many on the left
in 1992 precisely because he hammered this argument home
(even if he had not always lived up to the standard he set
during that campaign). The point here is simply that the two
phenomena—the emergence of a left-liberal identity-based
coalition and the hardening of a permanent governing class in
Washington whose rules constitute legal corruption—happened at the same time, with the result that, to many regular
Americans, the two appear to be intertwined. And they appear
that way because to some extent they are. The women's groups
are loathe to criticize Hillary Clinton for anything, even
though many questions surrounding her work for Madison
Guaranty Savings & Loan are clearly legitimate ones. There
are many examples, and in practically all cases, groups defend
individuals not on the basis of facts or criteria that uphold any
principles, but simply because of who they are. Perhaps the
best bit of proof of this, is the defense, in civil rights establish-

ment circles, of Commerce Secretary Ron Brown, a partner at one of Washington's most powerful law firms, Patton, Boggs, & Blow, who "happens to be" black. There is no better walking, breathing example of Washington cesspoolism than Brown. The head of the firm's trade division has stated that the firm will accept the first case that walks through the door, no matter what side of the issue. Brown's own many suspicious financial dealings—to say nothing of his willingness in previous years to serve as a U.S. representative of Haiti's Duvaliers, who in their day killed more black people than Bull Connor probably ever met—should have earned him the wrath of people of integrity, of whatever color, ages ago. Can anyone doubt that, had Brown been a white Republican, the left-liberal groups would have been mercilessly, and justifiably, on his tail? But as it happened, scarcely a peep was heard from civil rights leaders about Haiti, and when Brown came under attack for his finances, several defended his "integrity."

By no means is everyone on the left, it should be said, part of the liberal-left coalition described above. There are always exceptions and opposite tendencies in any movement. The Clintons have been the subject of ongoing debate on the left, and many radicals want nothing to do with them. Further, much left-wing activity in recent years—agitation for divestiture and sanctions against apartheid South Africa and opposition to Reagan's Central American policies—has been wholly to the good. But the arrival to power of the above coalition has moved those elements of the left that are involved in it far away from the mass of people and their concerns. It is, as I've noted, a left that is not organized around class politics, as the left was in previous times, but around issues of cultural identity. At this point, those issues must be examined more closely.

Chapter 3

E UNUM PLURIBUS

The Politics of Identity

What is identity politics? I've used the phrase up to this point without really defining it. It means, in essence, exactly what it says: a politics based on personal identity, as opposed to doctrine or philosophical worldview or, as the postmodernists sometimes say, "meta-narratives." Meta-narratives can be roughly defined as philosophical systems that seek to explain human and social behavior in world-historical terms, such as Marxism and, especially, Enlightenment-based universal humanism (the former is, in some respects, an offshoot of the latter).

Enlightenment universalism, of course, is the philosophical bedrock not only of the United States but of advanced Western society as a whole; the ideas of Locke and Hume and Voltaire and Jefferson and Paine remain the ideas that bind these countries together and that animate their sense of mission and progress. Identity politics, by and large, rejects these ideas. It holds that it's not universal rights and bonds—which, to identity advocates, are chimerical—that elevate people and give them power, but their own particular histories and involuntary affiliations—be they cultural, racial, ethnic, or gender-based—that enable them to act politically.

As such, the concept runs counter to the nation's most dearly held claim about itself: that we are a nation founded on "self-evident" principles. We are taught as schoolchildren that all people are "created equal" and are "endowed with certain unalienable rights," as Thomas Jefferson's Declaration of Independence put it. This is our ideal and our one true national religion, an ideal by which America, in Ralph Waldo Emerson's words, stands as an "asylum of all nations" in which "the energy of Irish, Germans, Swedes, Poles, and Cossacks, and all the European tribes—of the Africans, and of the Polynesians, will construct a new race . . . as vigorous as the new Europe which came out of the smelting pot of the Dark Ages." This sort of language has been invoked by politicians of both conservative and liberal stripe. For the former (Pat Robertson, say), it is all too often a blunt instrument used against *any* challenge to traditional notion of Americanism, while the latter (Arthur Schlesinger, Jr.) tend to be more accommodating of such challenges while still insisting that the ideal of the universal melting pot is put at grave risk by a politics of difference. And despite the fact that, as I showed in the previous chapter, liberals and even some conservatives play the identity card because it's such an easy way to buy off certain constituencies, at bottom twentieth-century liberalism and conservatism both profess faith in universalism as the only true way.

Identity politics eschews this in favor of, in the phrase of academic Charles Taylor, "the politics of recognition," that is, the demand for recognition—for respect and, concomitantly, for rights—by "subaltern" groups. And so, for identity politics, *e pluribus unum* is not an unrealized ideal. It is, instead, a sham and a lie, designed to keep certain groups—not people or citizens, but groups—down. And there are ways in which the argument is difficult to rebut. Even those who take the too sanguine view that, in the wake of the civil rights legislation of the '60s and other changes in American society, all past wrongs are now righted and we've achieved a state of social equality. must concede that universal rights, for the first century or more of the republic's history, did not embrace: black people, most of whom were counted not as citizens but as property; indigenous people (that is, those indigenous people who remained standing after the settlers and expansionists were through with them), their property stolen, herded onto reservations that resembled nothing so much as benign concentration camps; and women, who could not vote until 1920 and could not, with small exceptions, pursue roles of economic self-maintenance until very recently.

Picture a black woman living in any American city—North, South, wherever—at any time in the country's history until the last few years; she would want to hear precious little talk of universal rights. Or stop to wonder how black people must feel, still, on the Fourth of July. Their ancestors did not come over here to pursue a dream, and they were emphatically not welcomed onto Ellis Island by the inspiring sight of Lady Liberty in the harbor; they came to Norfolk or Annapolis or wherever, and were delivered straight to the auction block. "What is your Fourth of July to me?" Frederick Douglass asked. The holiday, indeed, is piquant: in some American cities in the late 1800s, blacks, seen as having no legitimate stake in the affair, were banned from attending Fourth of July celebrations.

Identity politics sees the world through these striations and would demand, for example, that the following question be asked of the above sentence: seen *by whom?* Well, by those who made such rules. And who were they? Well, the people in power. Yes, and they were? They were white men. And so history begins to appear to us differently, not as a single people creating a destiny but as groups of oppressed people struggling to forge their own destiny and identity in opposition to those few who exercised power over them. And those few have, throughout most of the country's history and with some small exceptions, always come from the same stable. Writing in *Tikkun*, the feminist critic Ellen Willis worked up a useful definition of identity politics, which she found to be based on the premise

> that membership in an oppressed group (in my case, as a woman or a Jew) determines my legitimacy as a political person, the validity of my political ideas, and indeed, my moral right to express them. Conversely, it assumes that as a member of a dominant group or majority (white, middle-class, heterosexual, able-bodied, etc.), I am morally bound to take political direction from the oppressed, since my experience, permeated as it is with privilege, can only steer me wrong.

Identity politics is "new" to America, having obtained currency in the last 25 years or so. But in truth, identity politics and Enlightenment universalism are coevals and have existed in tension for 200 years. In 1790, the French National Assembly voted for the first time to permit Jews to be full citizens of the Republic, provided they shed the "humiliating signs which designate them as Jews." Losing identity, that is, was the price of participation, of becoming universal. In early nineteenth-century Europe, in Germany in particular, Romantic thinkers such as Herder and Schiller sought to deny the Enlightenment's primacy (after all, it was mostly the distrusted French who were carrying on about universal rights) and establish the idea of a German nation and a German *volk*. In America, the political history of the republic was from the start a history of groups asserting political power, through the franchise, through protest, what have you. There has always been identity politics, in other words; it just wasn't called that. We tend to think of the Bostonians and Philadelphians and New Yorkers who ruled the nation in its early days as nothing more or less than, simply, Americans or early Americans. But were they not possessed of a particular identity as wealthy Anglo-Saxon Protestants? Surely Andrew Jackson's ascent to the presidency asserted the political identity of another group, the frontiersmen. Did not the mass immigration of Irish and other northern Europeans solidify their gains, as groups, against the opposition of the older WASP elite? What was the New Deal coalition except an amalgam of differently identified groups—southern whites, northern ethnics, those blacks who could vote, and all those self-identified as "the working class"? And urban machines were veritable identity factories—in New York City, the Irish, Italian, the Jew; in Chicago, the Irish, the Pole, the Slav, the Italian.

So there's no use pretending that identity politics is something brand new, something deviant from American experience. But there is a key difference. The old identity politics amounted to little more than political coalition-building among different groups. Irish and Italians during the New Deal may have expressed their electoral power as groups, but in the end what they wanted most was to assimilate, to be like everybody else, to be common rather than distinct. They didn't demand rights as Irish people or Italians; they demanded their rights, in the main, as newly minted Americans. And while they kept pretty much to themselves culturally, living together and maintaining certain rituals from the Old World, over time the New World incorporated some of those rituals and customs into its fabric.

In today's identity politics, people seek rights not as Americans but as members of self-identified groups. Note, in Willis's definition, that membership in such a group *determines* legitimacy—it does not "help shape" or "assist in forming," it determines. Thus has assimilation given way in the watchword sweepstakes to "authenticity," a badge of being that carries the implication that those who are not in an authentic condition of being oppressed can't possibly understand the problems faced by those who are (this implication is often made unmistakeably explicit in actual conversations about politics, as when one is accused of being a "straight white male" as though that's equivalent to "landlord" or "phone company"). Identity, today, is not just about electoral politics and election-time coalition-building, but about a whole panoply of social and cultural activities, from one's sexual practices to what music one enjoys to how one dresses. Identity-based organizing has led to demands for and the creation of specialized departments and areas of study in higher education. In the academy, books on feminist theory and queer theory proliferated in recent years, while on the mass market, books by young writers of color—books that need not be about anything but their experiences as young writers of color—are all the rage. Ask someone from such a group today what she or he thinks on a given subject, and the answer will likely begin, As a gay man, I think . . . or, As a physically challenged African-American woman, I believe. . . . Within today's left, identity is, if not everything, then at least the dock from which all investigations are launched.

This is by no means all bad, and in fact many developments that are rooted in identity politics have had a salutary effect on the broader culture. The women's movement has given American women many opportunities, and gay men and lesbians see much more tolerance than they once did. The writing of history has changed dramatically for the better, and we're more aware of the cultural biases in our history and national mythology. Think of the arts and literature in recent years; would Amy Tan, Alice Walker, Terry McMillan, Maya Angelou, Darrell Pinckney, Laura Esquivel, Sandra Cisneros, Jamaica Kincaid, and dozens of other writers have been able to flourish as they have if they'd been born, say, in the 1920s? A few of them perhaps, but no more than a few. And unlike the cabinet members of the previous chapter, Walker et al. are not just symbols drawn from the same managerial class as the white men who preceded them. They *do* come from diverse backgrounds, and they have something unique to add to our common conception of America, things to say about this country and its culture that are just as interesting and useful— to all of us, not just to members of their races—as the insights of Faulkner and Twain. All this is changing, not by accident, but because people have worked to make the changes.

So the impact on American culture of the search for identity and diversity has been much to the good. But in political terms, identity politics has proved to be a disaster for the left. Identity politics places a relentless focus on difference, on categories of groups and their special agendas, and allows for no analysis of what unites people. Paradoxically, it also reduces people within those groups to a kind of bland sameness that has nothing to do with how the world really is: people are complex, and they simply don't live their lives according to rigid categories of race or gender. This duality—the promotion of intergroup difference and intragroup sameness—serves to harden the lines between the races and the genders, rendering cross-racial coalition-building—the left's only hope of regaining even a modicum of power—virtually impossible; after all, why sit down and work with someone who simply cannot understand? And so identity politics, in its most ossified form, becomes much like what it despises: whereas racism and sexism for decades caused blacks and women to be excluded, authenticity today demands the exclusion of those who have no credentials as being historically oppressed. No matter which side builds the wall, it ends up in the same place.

The possibility of coalition-building across lines of race (and gender and sexual orientation) is something to which all identity advocates pay thundering lip service, but few of them go beyond it. Most essays that explore identities close with an obligatory two or three paragraphs proclaiming the paramount importance of everyone getting together, but very few of these essays ever take the time to suggest practical ideas about how to do it.

The personal is political. This catchphrase of identity politics that originated with feminism implies that identity is all, that ideas and argument are nullities, and that to think independently and perhaps reach unorthodox conclusions is therefore to put one's authenticity and group membership at risk. It also implies that the nonpersonal isn't; one need only mull that over for a few moments to understand the woeful implications for those (working-class whites, housewives, churchgoers, Kurds) whose personal experiences are not those of the anointed group. Thus are many potential allies simply written off, and many concerns and causes that should preoccupy the left—concerns that would help build the kind of coalitions referred to above—ignored.

The result is a left that's isolated into ever smaller compartments from which there is no escape. This left can claim a few accomplishments, but it cannot make the claim, despite all the talk of "empowerment," that it has improved peoples' material situations. The lives of poor black people, for example, have simply gotten worse in the years that identity has triumphed; and now, for the first time in our modern history, laws are being written that penalize poor women for having babies. It's no accident, in other words, that the right has taken over the country just as the left has permitted itself to disintegrate into ever more discrete race- and gender-based camps. If the left is to escape the box it has put itself in, the passing away of this sort of politics must be the first precondition.

By 1966 and 1967, the disagreements among the groups that made up the New Left were growing into genuine schisms. Kwame Toure (Stokely Carmichael, then) and other young black leaders decided that whites could no longer be members of the Student Non-Violent Coordinating Committee, the black-led student group that had done so much to force integration in the South. The phrase Black Power was first used in an exhortatory way in late 1966; one month before that, the Black Panthers had released their party platform and program. The last paragraph of that platform comprised the second paragraph of the Declaration of Independence almost in its entirety, but was less a tribute to universalism than a caustic send-up of it. Black leadership was no longer satisfied with the goal of integration that seemed so slow in coming, and so the more radical rhetoric of the Panthers and of the late Malcolm X and his followers gained appeal, especially after the riots of 1967 and the assassination of Dr. King, which sparked further rioting. A gathering of New Left groups known as the National Conference for New Politics, held in Chicago over Labor Day weekend, 1967, to unify the movement, merely ended up showing how far black and white had drifted apart. The black leaders in attendance demanded that the body adopt a resolution condemning Israeli aggression in the Six Day War. The Six Day War and Israel's occupation of the West Bank and Gaza were well worth condemning, but they had next to nothing to do with the proceedings at hand, except that most of the white activists there were Jewish. The resolution was, as French author Michel Feher wrote, "an open provocation," but it was approved instantly, setting the tone for the white left's patronizing attitude toward black activism in the years to come.

Something else happened at the NCNP meeting. Shula-mith Firestone and Jo Freeman, two early feminist leaders, drafted a resolution demanding that the convention endorse "the revamping of marriage, divorce, and property laws" and the "complete control by women over their own bodies," among other things. They argued long and hard to get the conference to agree to consider the resolution, which it finally did. But when its turn came, another milder resolution—written, interestingly enough, by Madlyn Murray O'Hair—was substituted on the sly. This event, combined with other stirrings taking place around the same time, encouraged the women of the New Left to break off from the broader movement and go it on their own. Some of the thinking wasn't especially new—cultural radical Victoria Woodhull, describing marriage, had written back in 1874 of her wish "to stab it to the heart, so that its decaying carcass may be buried." What was new, though, was the possibility of a movement.

And in Greenwich Village, New York, it seemed at first that the police raid on a gay bar called the Stonewall Inn one June night in 1969 would be just like the many hundreds that preceded it. But for some reason, the "nellys" and drag queens who hung out there decided they'd had enough and refused to run for cover or go quietly to booking, as they'd done in the past. No one is sure to this day what set the riot off, but everyone seemed to know immediately that a decisive moment had come: "It was just like Newark," recalled gay leader Jim Fouratt. What had been a moderate and accommodating "homophile movement" that used persuasion and argument to make its case was transformed after that night into the gay liberation movement, a radicalized tendency that would use confrontation and make demands.

I won't trace in any great detail the histories of these movements; that is done thoroughly in many other sources. The point here, though, is to evoke the times and context in which identity politics first came to dominate thought and action on the left. One can see from how the New Left's leaders—white, male, and straight—neglected concerns that they didn't consider their own that new causes and movements led by women and gays were necessary. "Fuck off, left," Firestone wrote in 1969. "You can examine your navel by yourself from now on." Further, one can see from the Six Day War episode just how profoundly white guilt about racism overwhelmed rigorous analysis, the application of which would certainly have led to the conclusion that a resolution condemning Israel was either superfluous or at the very least in need of honest discussion. Remember, also, what was happening simultaneously: the white working and middle classes were becoming more conservative, and the populist politics that the left had used to gain their support in the past had become the province of the right and of Nixon's silent majority. And so the left more or less just quit worrying about broader public opinion and trying to assuage it. Left-wing activist politics became not only increasingly splintered but also increasingly disassociated from a larger population that, as far as the various New Left groups were concerned, was still living in the Stone Age.

In addition, black and women's magazines and newspapers, both mainstream and underground, along with academic journals, began to appear in abundance. Both groups undertook not only to awaken others—mainly leftists and liberals who weren't "getting it"—to the cause, but also, plainly, to shock, traduce, slander, and defame. H. Rap Brown, the new SNCC leader who had once said he "just might shoot Ladybird," published an autobiography called *Die Nigger Die!* Firestone's *Dialectic of Sex* proclaimed (optimistically, in retrospect) the revolutionary nature of feminism. Not to generalize too much, it's fair to say that the early literature of the black power and women's liberation movements was on the whole heated and emotional in the extreme. Robin Morgan's famous essay,

"Goodbye To All That," which originally appeared in the underground newspaper *Rat* in 1970, is typical:

> Let it all hang out. Let it seem bitchy, catty, dykey, frustrated, crazy, Solanisesque, nutty, frigid, ridiculous, bitter, embarrassing, man-hating, libelous, pure, unfair, envious, intuitive, low-down, stupid, petty, liberating. We are the women that men have warned us about.

("Solanisesque" refers, misspelling notwithstanding, to Valerie Solanas, a habitué of Andy Warhol's Factory who, in 1967, had formed SCUM—the Society for Cutting Up Men. She made good on the threat, if not the specific method of delivery, by pumping Warhol full of lead in 1968. He lived, and she served two years.)

But there was analysis in addition to anger. As noted in the introduction, identity-inclined radicals of this era looked to French thinkers whose ideas became associated with the convulsive 1968 student uprisings in France: Michel Foucault, with his emphasis on marginal social groups; Jacques Derrida, with his emphasis on the oppressive nature of language; and Jacques Lacan, with his emphasis on eroticism and male power structures. Americans, being more inclined toward action than thought, as Paul Berman has noted, were considerably less high-flown, but the ideas of these French postmodernists did find their way over the next few years into the writings of many radical American intellectuals. They certainly came to serve as guides for radical politics and to dominate the radical academy. Foucault, especially, has been important, having influenced the turn away from universalizing strategies and toward a "micropolitics" that does not recognize a state with power. For Foucault, to fight the state is to accept its legitimacy as the holder of power; in his studies of penal systems, psychiatric hospitals, and the like, he asserts that power reposes not in the state but in "the mechanisms of disciplinary coercion" that are to be found in various social arrangements—although Foucault tended not to make much of the difference between a prisoner, say, and a fellow with a nine- to-five job. Obviously, this is a very shorthand rendering, but suffice it to say that the appeal to out-groups of his "anarchism/nihilism," as Michael Walzer has labeled it, lay in its strong challenge to all accepted notions of rationality and morality.

The French philosophers' general belief that power was not an instrument of the state and thus could not be changed through rebellion or revolution fit nicely with the emerging identity movements' view that class struggle was not the name of the game. In other words, the old idea of proletarian revolution was useless; what became important were a thousand little revolutions, not against a state but against a thousand little oppressors. From this point on, class would no longer be the basis of radical analysis; power relationships would be. Thus, the late '60s saw a repudiation of the most central tenet of radical thought since its beginnings some 150 years before. For black activists, racism became more important than the exploitation of workers by capitalists; for women, sexism. Robin Morgan addressed both points in her essay:

> Two evils predate capitalism and have been clearly able to survive and post-date socialism: sexism and racism. Women were the first property when the Primary Contradiction occurred: when one half of the human species decided to subjugate the other half, because it was "different," alien, the Other. From there it was an easy enough step to extend the Other to someone of different skin shade, different height or weight or language—or strength to resist. Goodbye to those simple-minded optimistic dreams of socialist equality all our good socialist brothers want us to believe. How liberal a politics that is!

Thus, we can say with reasonable precision that 1970 or thereabouts was the moment when the American left cashiered traditional class-based politics for a new variant in which race and gender were preeminent.

Not everyone agreed on everything, of course. The new identity movements remained divided between liberal and radical wings; Brown's and Firestone's less incendiary brethren and sistren went off to become McGovernites, and in fact, the liberals probably outnumbered the radicals. Within the radical movement itself, debates were endless. Radical feminism was torn from the start by arguments about feminism's relationship to socialism; according to Alice Echols, one of its chroniclers, the feminist movement is "virtually impossible to understand . . . without referring to the movement's divided beginnings." To read this history is to read of doctrinal fights that make the early Soviet party congresses look like afternoon teas. There were arguments over socialism, style, make-up, music, men, the penis, and whether or not women living collectively should wear one another's clothes. There were intense fights over lesbianism. NOW kept gay women out of organizational office, while the more radical groups were riven by such questions as whether sleeping with men was succumbing to the patriarchy, since men's domination of women was presumed to be based on sex, and whether the alternative of sleeping with women was not just mimetic of male-female coupling and thus itself compromising, leaving celibacy and self-arousal as the only true path to freedom. That's how things were in those days.

But divided as feminists may have been, one basic belief united them: the old, class-based politics wasn't relevant anymore. The same is largely true of black thinkers over the past 25 years, during which time they've been engaged in intensive investigations into the nature of black identity. The looming question—or at least one that seems to frame much discussion of the topic—is the one W.E.B. DuBois famously posed in 1903 in his seminal book, *The Souls of Black Folk*. DuBois wrote of the Negro's inherent "double-consciousness," his "sense of always looking at one's self through the eyes of others, of measuring one's soul by the tape of a world that looks on in amused contempt and pity. One ever feels his twoness—an American, a Negro; two souls, two thoughts, two unreconciled strivings; two warring ideals in one dark body, whose dogged strength alone keeps it from being torn asunder." Could those two identities, DuBois wondered, ever be joined?

As racial strife grew, the answers became ever more pessimistic. The poet and essayist Nikki Giovanni sees DuBois, who in other passages distinguished between the "talented tenth" of the black population and the other 90 percent, as the father of black conservatives like Clarence Thomas; she prefers the much more explicitly nationalist Marcus Garvey. (It must be noted that DuBois, who in 1909 had helped found the biracial National Association for the Advancement of Colored People, later gave up on integration, espoused Pan-Africanism, and, matching deed to word, moved to Ghana, where he lived out the final years of his life.) Still other critics, like Molefi Kete Asante, the founder of the contemporary Afrocentrism movement, see this double-consciousness as an illusion: "I have always known that my heritage was not the same as whites." Asante heads the African American Studies department at Temple University. Afrocentrism, with its "proofs" that the Egyptians were a black race that invented just about everything short of the internal combustion engine and had it all stolen by the rapacious Greeks, was bound to flourish in an atmosphere of racial nationalism—and, to be fair, in an atmosphere in which white society does in fact downplay many of the real contributions of black people and cultures. The fact that whites scoff at Afrocentrism, of course, just serves to reinforce its validity to adherents.

Race consciousness pervaded feminism as well. By the mid-1970s, many black women looked upon the white leaders of the feminist movement in much the same way that Asante looked at the whites he grew up around in rural Georgia. Many black feminists came to see the feminist movement as a largely middle-class, white movement that wasn't addressing their particular needs and concerns (they were right, actually). In April 1977, a group of Boston-based radical black women called the Combahee River Collective issued a statement criticizing the larger feminist movement and announcing, "We believe that the most profound and potentially most radical politics come directly out of our own identity."

These paths continued to narrow and diverge throughout the '70s and '80s. Choose a nonwhite ethnicity, combine it with a sexual practice or a physical condition, and there probably exists a movement to match. One could walk down these roads much further, but the point has been made: what was once a reasonably coherent movement, full of its share of disagreements but united around the basic principles of support for civil rights, belief in class as the basis of political analysis, and commitment to personal liberation, has spun out into many separate and smaller movements with no coherent agenda at all. And personal liberation, which ought properly to mean the right of all people to pursue the fullest lives they possibly can, free from want and from state interference in their personal choices, these days often means the "right" to do whatever you please whenever you please, all the more so if it subverts authority or makes middle-class whites upset. This can be seen in the twisting of the concept of rights from the protection of citizens against state intrusion to the provision of legal support for any conceivable kind of human activity (some people choose to undergo sex-change operations, for example; does this "identity" transfer into a "right"?).

Certainly there have been positive developments, in addition to those in the broader culture mentioned above. We could not, today, imagine a Congress with virtually no black representatives, as was the case, really, until the 1970s, or with no women. Gay men and lesbians hold political office in places where those constituencies have political power, and Latinos, a growing population in most parts of the country, are also starting to have real influence in American domestic politics. No one on the left would want to argue against these gains, but 25 years on, we've reached a point that can only be called ridiculous, if not actually destructive.

Consider the case of transracial adoptions. Today in the United States, around 50,000 black children await adoption into loving homes—children, in large part, who are victims of urban poverty. No huge number of parents is rushing to take in these children, so one would think that any decent, caring home would be welcomed by the foster agencies. Not so. The National Association of Black Social Workers, which obviously has some leverage in the question, opposes transracial adoptions in any form, because a black child in a white home will supposedly be deprived of his or her proper culture. Congress, weighing the question in 1993, would not go so far as the NABSW wanted, but the Senate did come up with a bill that stated a preference for "racial matching" and allowed for 110 transracial adoptions only as a last resort. This bill was the work, incidentally, of some of the Senate's most liberal members: Ohio's Howard Metzenbaum (now retired), along with Massachusetts's Ted Kennedy and Chris Dodd of Connecticut.

It's hard to know where to begin to describe the sadness of this. A white couple shows the compelling courage to raise a black child, only to be told they're the wrong color. Children, meanwhile, wait and suffer. The idea that racial culture is everything is upheld, while the ideal of integration, of an American culture that can rise above racial categories, is crushed into dust. Black racialism and white liberal patronism combine to create a disaster both moral and practical—and reproduce the very world that, not so long ago, enlightened thinkers unanimously opposed. As legal scholar Randall Kennedy writes:

> When *The New York Times* editorializes today that "clearly, matching adoptive parents with children of the same race is a good idea," we should recall that not very long ago it was believed in some parts of this nation that "clearly" it was a good idea to match people of the same race in separate but equal parks, hospitals, prisons, cemeteries, telephone booths, trains, and practically every other place one can imagine—all for the asserted purpose of accommodating the underlying racial sentiments of those who opposed "racial mixing."

Thus does identity become indistinguishable from that which it supposedly arose to combat. The racist stereotype that all blacks are alike has been nudged aside by the supposedly radical notion that all blacks should be alike in order to be authentic black people. How different, in the end, are those two postulates?

The worst case, in racial terms, is the credibility afforded by many black leaders to Louis Farrakhan, leader of the Nation of Islam. Farrakhan has no place as a spokesman in a multicultural, democratic society. And yet black leaders, in the name of their shared racial identity, at best try to avoid commenting on the matter and at worst defend him. When former NAACP chief Benjamin Chavis joined former Maryland Congressman and current NAACP head Kweisi Mfume, then chairman of the Congressional Black Caucus, to forge their infamous "sacred covenant" with Farrakhan, scarcely a word of criticism was heard from most other black public figures.

However, two admirable black public figures did speak out. Congressman Major Owens, who represents Brooklyn's Crown Heights and adjacent neighborhoods, took a stand immediately: "No more time should be wasted on negotiations with

hatemongers and rank opportunists. Reject [Khalid] Muham-
mad and Farrakhan . . . We must denounce the enemy. We
must isolate the enemy. We must ignore any devious future
overtures from the enemy." Owens is no apologist for anyone or
anything; he's one of the most left-leaning members of the
House of Representatives who, in his personal history, is just
about as steeped in multiracial coalition politics as anyone can
be. Like all black Americans, he knows racism firsthand and
knows how painful being black in the United States can be; in
college in Atlanta in the 1950s, he fell in love with a white
woman and they had to leave Georgia to be able to marry legally. Another figure who spoke up was Michael Meyers, head
of the New York Civil Rights Coalition. Appeals based on race,
he wrote, on "empowerment through skin color, identity politics and the denigrating of others' cultures are dangerously
infectious" and cannot be allowed to succeed. Meyers was in-
strumental in the push for the removal of Chavis and William
Gibson as executive director and chairman of the board of that
organization because of their embrace of Farrakhan and some
other dubious practices.

What has their frankness got them? Meyers is considered in
New York "progressive" circles to be a crank, a reactionary, a
tool of the white establishment, or worse. The only local
forum in which he can get his writings published on a regular
basis is the conservative *New York Post*. Owens, who has represented his district in Congress since 1982 and who was virtually assured a seat for life until he spoke out against Farrakhan,
is looked upon with scorn by many black activists and will undoubtedly face challenges for the foreseeable future from more
nationalistic blacks. And, sad to say, he could be beaten by
someone willing to excoriate him as a sellout.

All this merely laid the groundwork for the 1995 Million
Man March on Washington, D.C. An event that was in many

ways beautiful—peaceful, uplifting, wholly positive for many of the men involved—carried the horrible downside of giving Farrakhan prestige. I've no doubt that very few men who marched did so because of allegiance to Farrakhan; they and the march's many defenders insisted that it was possible to separate the march from Farrakhan, and to some extent that's true. But people like Jesse Jackson and Cornel West, both of whom participated, should have been able to recognize that their presence lent Farrakhan legitimacy. More important, they should be able to see that the elevation of Farrakhan is the best present the Christian Coalition and the Liberty Lobby could ever hope to receive.

The same logic that leads to the acceptance of a Farrakhan enables any self-identified group to demand of all outsiders who support it the backing without reservation of every single aspect of the group's agenda. Recall the second part of Ellen Willis's definition quoted earlier in this chapter: membership in a "dominant group or majority" renders one "morally bound to take political direction from the oppressed." By this measure, to be white and to object to Farrakhan, or to argue that Shakespeare is enduringly relevant to all students of literature whatever their background, is to become the oppressor. And so any well-intended questioning of strategy or purpose or larger aim is taken as an attack; what ensues is not dialogue, but name-calling and vilification. And to the charge of racism or sexism or homophobia there is no possible answer; it's the multicultural equivalent of the age-old question, When did you stop beating your wife?

It is not my, or anyone's, responsibility to support every action these movements undertake. I believe that gay people should be protected by federal civil rights legislation, and I believe that gay couples who can reasonably demonstrate that they are committed to spending their lives together should enjoy the same legal benefits—the option of filing taxes and owning property jointly, of adopting each other's children, and what have you—as straight married couples. But I also find it deeply offensive, though I'm not particularly religious, when gay activists in New York storm St. Patrick's Cathedral, expose themselves on Fifth Avenue, stage "kiss-ins," or desecrate the host—apparently, the right to "respect" does not extend to respect for the customs and traditions of the "oppressor." What do such actions accomplish, aside from alienating potential sympathizers among rank-and-file Catholics (and many surveys have shown that Catholics are less conservative than their leaders)? None of this makes me homophobic; it merely means that I have a working mind, and I am free to reach my own conclusions about what I believe is right and wrong. But today's left utterly fails to recognize this.

There are signs that identity's stranglehold on leftist politics is abating. Perhaps the battering the left has taken in the culture wars, combined with the right's undeniable triumph at the polls, has finally caused the left to rethink these questions. Kennedy, West (his role in the march aside), Henry Louis Gates, Jr., and K. Anthony Appiah are among the African American thinkers who have tried in their writings to find a place where the particular and the universal can meet. Appiah, who is gay as well, has written that "the bureaucratic categories of identity . . . come up short before the vagaries of actual peoples' lives," although he also argues that identity politics has transformative powers for group members that should not be ignored. These thinkers and others don't agree with one another right down the line, and for all I know may strongly disagree with my views, but the point is that they've taken positions that acknowledge the need for thinking and acting according to principles higher than those biological.

People will always organize themselves around group interests. But when the group interest pushes everything else to the side and makes demands on others that are intolerant, unreasonable, and against the spirit of critical inquiry—which the left, in better days, held dear—then something has gone terribly wrong. And until it's fixed, nothing will change.

Chapter 4

QUESTIONS, BUT NEVER ANSWERS
Welfare

The first three chapters have sought to describe the left's current weakness in general terms. The decline of the movement from broad-based mass organizations into small and fractured groups, and the plain dwindling of the number of those who identify themselves as leftist; the left's decreasing empathy with the conditions faced by working-class Americans; the alliance of much of the active left, beginning in the 1970s, with a liberal elite that itself was failing to represent the interests of many working people; the rise of identity politics, with its consuming emphasis on intergroup differences and intragroup sameness, which has all too often rendered the left divided within itself, isolated and politically weak, unable and unwilling to articulate the common goals and needs of the people at large. Of course, not everything about the left's predicament is the left's fault, and this book would be incomplete without at least a mention of the fact that the left has faced an uphill battle in this country, fundamentally because it opposes the agenda of corporate America. Corporate America has about ten thousand times the influence and money the left has, and thus will always be in a position to disseminate its propaganda far more effectively than we ever could. This circumstance is so obvious it need not be dwelt on, and anyway, moaning about the fact is roughly as useful as complaining about the weather.

This chapter and the three that follow move to the specific. These four chapters will serve as case studies of four major policy areas in which the left has, to put it bluntly, lost the argument: welfare, immigration, affirmative action, and health care. Some will object that it is too much to say at this point that these arguments have been lost; affirmative action, at least as of this writing, is holding its own, even though polls tend to show that large majorities of Americans oppose racial and gender preferences. But one thing that cannot be denied is that on all these issues—and if they're not the four most important domestic issues as we finish off the century, they're certainly four issues on which the left must develop answers—the debate is being played out largely on the right's terms: welfare will be scaled back, possibly eviscerated; immigration will likely be curtailed, and benefits to illegals and even legals, if some have their way, will face the knife; affirmative action, though granted a stay of execution by President Clinton's broad endorsement of it in July 1995, nevertheless sits on death row; and the health care battle was lost, first with the Clinton administration's opposition to the left's preferred alternative of a single-payer plan, and then with the failure of Clinton's mishmash of a plan.

Provided the Republicans retain control of the Congress, and especially if they win the White House, we can see now what welfare reform will look like in the late 1990s, and it's an ugly sight. The folding of many federal programs into large and highly discretionary block grants for the states will be disastrous for poor people. First, local business and corporate elites at the state level have even more control over politicians than they do in Washington—states typically have less stringent campaign finance and lobbying disclosure requirements, for example, meaning that huge political contributions and other forms of access are never revealed to the public. Second, as the Democratic Party tumbles, more and more states and localities are governed by conservatives. So we can be pretty sure that most states will slash benefits, reflexively invoking the language (personal responsibility, illegitimacy, etc.) we all know so well. All but those few states where large numbers of poor and high costs of living dictate some modicum of generosity will probably become engaged in what we might call antibidding wars—that is to say, states will continually seek to make their benefits lower that those of neighboring states so that poor people from the latter will have no incentive to move in. Without federal minimums, why not? Surely there's at least a conservative or two out there hoping that, if all goes well, people will soon be emigrating *to* Mexico rather than immigrating from it.

We also have a sense of just how far Bill Clinton will bend in order to enter his reelection campaign able to brag that he's "ended welfare as we know it." His collapse on welfare in the fall of 1995, when he essentially accepted the major tenets of Republican welfare reform, will stand as one of the most craven acts of his presidency (his subsequent veto of the GOP's welfare legislation seems less likely to change the debate fundamentally than simply to delay the inevitable). And of course, most Democrats signed on as well, so heated is the general rush to claim some sort of victory on this front. Daniel Patrick Moynihan rightly expressed scorn for his president and fellow Democrats for folding so easily, but Moynihan—whatever one thinks of his notions, a knowledgeable man on these matters—wasn't able to do much to rally opposition before the fact.

Whatever the final outcome, we know that welfare reform has been a long time in coming. There was opposition to welfare—and, as we shall see, not just from the right—practically from its inception, or at least from the moment it was expanded, in the early 1960s, from a mainly temporary program to support widows and certain indigents into the broad federal relief program it is today. There were Johnson-era efforts to tinker with it; Nixon tried to change it, in some ways actually for the better; Ford and, more notably, Carter had welfare reform legislation in the works. It took the Reagan landslide to provide fertile ground for thinkers like Charles Murray (whose 1984 book *Losing Ground* blamed welfare for illegitimacy and black cultural structures) and Lawrence Mead (one of the first serious proponents of workfare whose writings on the subject appeared often in *Commentary* and other conservative journals) could drive the issue to the center of the national discussion. Much of Reagan's rhetoric, of course—about people buying vodka with their foodstamps and the like—was vile and absurdly exaggerated, but he got away with it. Meanwhile, the conservatives had had their knives drawn early on, while the liberals for the most part were befuddled, not quite sure what to do.

Where has the left been in all this? Out of town, mostly. Certainly the left, as we shall see, has refused by and large even to participate in discussions about moving people from the welfare rolls into jobs. Indeed, the left's greatest "contribution" to the welfare debate has been the opposite: put more people on the dole. The welfare debate of the past few years provides a stark example of one of the left's great problems of recent vintage, namely, its ability to critique everyone else's ideas with a vengeance but fail to offer substantive ideas of its own. Not that left analyses of welfare fail to provide any ways to address the problem. They do, and they are often correct in the abstract. But usually the left's proposals are vague and pietistic: good jobs at good wages, real opportunity as opposed to the sham opportunity that work programs provide. Nothing with any meat to it, really, and virtually no discussion of realistic strategies to achieve goals.

As to the left's critiques, while to my mind they are in many ways correct, they nevertheless do not provide an answer to the right in any substantive way. And as the years pass, the critiques get more and more defensive and hostile, with the result that conversation on the subject is driven down almost to the level of the playground. As left and right persist in shouting at each other, the inadequacy of the explanations on both sides simply becomes more and more evident—another manifestation how the categories left and right have become increasingly otiose. The right says it's all about personal responsibility and poor people's behavior; the left says it's all about root economic and social causes. Each denies with vehemence the other side's stance. The fact is—and most people believe and common sense tells us—that the truth is in the middle: poor people face social and economic obstacles the rest of us don't and poor black people, especially, have faced unspeakable, horrific discrimination of a sort that makes it remarkable that they continue to strive forward at all. Recognizing this does not mean, however, that all discussion of behavior is necessarily out of bounds. Teenagers—black, white, male, female, whatever—having children they can't or won't support *is* a problem, and a crucial one, because nearly three-quarters of teenage girls who bear children end up on welfare, some for short periods, some for long. The response to the problem need not be a punitive one, though. Just as important, the motivations of everyone seeking to change this behavior are not uniformly racist or patriarchal, as the left often asserts.

To understand the contemporary debate we must go back, again, to the 1960s, when the current discourse began to assume its form. We could begin in any number of places, but a logical starting point is the release of the Moynihan Report in 1965. Daniel Patrick Moynihan, now a U.S. senator from New York, was an assistant secretary of labor in the Johnson administration when he (as chief author) produced a report for the president entitled "The Negro Family: The Case for National Action." It seems odd, given the persistent low reputation of the report and its author among many civil rights figures, black activists, and leftists of various stripes, but the report was actually intended to lay the groundwork for the most massive attack on poverty the nation had ever seen. It led directly to LBJ's noted Howard University commencement speech of June 1965, the one that contains the famous quote often used today to defend affirmative action and other public benefactions toward minorities: "You do not take a person who, for years, has been hobbled by chains and liberate him, bring him up to the starting line of a race and then say, 'you are free to compete with all the others,' and still justly believe that you have been completely fair." (Those who today loathe Moynihan but quote that speech may wish to recall that he co-wrote it, with LBJ aide Richard Goodwin.) That speech, in turn, led to the 1966 White House report, "To Fulfill These Rights," which summarized the Johnson administration's antipoverty pledges. These were well-intended but hindered, to say the least, by the Moynihan controversy and by the redirection of antipoverty funds toward the creation of poverty—and far worse—in Indochina.

Since it's probably safe to assume that many people who despise (as well as those who defend) the Moynihan Report haven't read it and know only that it describes the "Negro

family" as "a tangle of pathology," a brief summary is in order.
Moynihan essentially argued that historical racism and economic pressures had created a family structure among poor
blacks that, veering from the middle-class tradition of a two-
parent, father-headed household, had served to ensure their
continued poverty by engendering cycles of illegitimacy from
which escape was difficult (though possible). He did invoke
the dastardly phrase four times, by my count, but the report
also made clear that the pathology in question was the result
of three hundred years of the most violent treatment any
group of people has ever visited on another in the civilized
world. Chapter III, "The Roots of the Problem," devotes sections to slavery ("indescribably worse than any recorded ser-
vitude, ancient or modern"), Reconstruction ("the Negro
male . . . became an object of intense hostility"), urbaniza-
tion, unemployment and poverty, and the wage system.

But if the brunt of Moynihan's argument, as two liberal
scholars put it at the time, was that "underemployment and
related poverty produce family breakdown"—a wholly unre-
markable thesis—it certainly didn't come out that way when
the report hit the press. In this respect, Moynihan perhaps deserves less scorn and the major columnists who interpreted the
report for their decision-making readers deserve more. First
the liberal Mary McGrory and later the conservative tandem
Rowland Evans and Robert Novak, all writing in *The Washington Post*, hailed the report and Johnson's Howard University
speech as showing (in Evans and Novak's words) that "broken
homes, illegitimacy, and female-oriented homes were central
to big-city Negro problems," and thus that blacks had to help
themselves first. These columns—which helped form the
opinions of lots of people in Washington—completely ignored
Chapter III and other sections of the report that clearly sought
to tie broken homes and the rest to a continuing history of discrimination and dislocation. The crucial difference between

what Moynihan wrote and what McGrory, Evans, and Novak wrote, in other words, was no less than the difference between white culpability and white exoneration.

It's clear, if Moynihan is to be taken at his word, that his intent was to introduce family structure as a legitimate concern of public policy, which it had not theretofore been, but to do so in a way that would compel national action on black poverty. Moynihan wrote a lengthy response to the controversy the report sparked in *Commentary* in 1967. In it, he asserted that he knew very well that mention of family structure would "arouse immediate interest," and he argued that "describing the plight of so many Negro families appeared the surest way to bring home the reality of their need." In particular, he believed that the possibility of federal programs aimed at strengthening families—and a guaranteed family income, even for families with the father living at home, was the main policy goal—would "enlist the support of the more conservative and tradition-oriented centers of power in American life whose enthusiasm for class legislation is limited indeed." So Moynihan was apparently making a political calculation: injecting family structure into the debate, he hoped, would give the idea of relieving black poverty broader legislative appeal than any aggressively redistributive legislation could ever hope to achieve.

Initially at least, reaction among civil rights activists was not wholly negative. The Howard speech, which also delved into the problems of family structure—and again, these were identified as resulting from racism—was well received in the civil rights world. Martin Luther King, Roy Wilkins, and Whitney Young had been shown a draft of the speech and had approved it. Later, Robert Carter of the NAACP praised the report and "could not understand the great shock" some expressed. Young said it "identified the same pathologies" as his own book had, although the title was unfortunate and stigmatizing. Bayard

Rustin criticized it for leaving its readers "with the view that this is a complete and perfectly true picture of the Negro families," although he thought labeling Moynihan a racist was "silly." King, diplomatically perhaps, saw Moynihan's analysis as offering "dangers and opportunities"—the opportunity to galvanize support and marshal resources, but the danger that "problems will be attributed to innate Negro weakness and used to justify, neglect and rationalize oppression."

Over the next few months, though, it was the dangers that civil rights leaders and Moynihan critics emphasized. Writing in *The Nation* in November 1965, William Ryan, a Boston psychologist who was associated with the Congress of Racial Equality, condemned the report under the headline "Savage Discovery": "The implicit point is that Negroes tolerate promiscuity, illegitimacy, one-parent families, welfare dependency, and everything else that is supposed to follow." Whether the report actually made that implicit point—and it strikes me as a defensive reading of the document—the line that Ryan drew hardened over the years into today's left/right divide. Hence, to the left, any suggestion that illegitimate births or matriarchal family structures may have something to do with poverty and a person's need for public assistance is taken as evidence that one is in bed with Moynihan and Charles Murray (to the left, they're scarcely distinguishable).

As noted above, the controversy over the report—in its wake, the White House conference that produced "To Fulfill These Rights" foundered—and the snowballing momentum of Vietnam stanched whatever commitment Johnson had previously had to addressing poverty and reforming welfare. The left's opposition to Vietnam also meant that its support for Johnson's domestic programs waned. The riots in Watts, which occurred shortly after the report was written, also slowed the momentum and gave grist to the Great Society's foes. By 1966, impatient with government, poor people began to organize themselves, first at a convention in Syracuse, New York, in January. The National People's War (on poverty) Council was ignored by liberal officials of the Johnson administration, by Governor Nelson Rockefeller's administration in New York, and by major civil rights groups, but it was the first large conference to bring together poor workers (Cesar Chavez led a delegation) and mothers receiving Aid to Families with Dependent Children, the program generally meant when we speak of welfare. The conference marked the first real attempt to alert welfare recipients to the benefit options, albeit limited, available to them—that is, to alert them to their rights.

By the spring of that year, the lineaments of a new movement would be clear. But the goal of this movement was not to move people off welfare; rather, it was to put more people on. The welfare rights movement—led on the ground by CORE's George Wiley and in print by Richard A. Cloward and Frances Fox Piven, both then at Columbia University—had as its improbable thesis that putting more people on the welfare rolls would force an urban political crisis that the nation's liberal politicians would have no choice but to deal with if they wanted to maintain Democratic supremacy in national politics. The following passage from their article "A Strategy to End Poverty," which appeared in *The Nation* in 1966, is so redolent of those dewy-eyed times, and has proven so breathtakingly wrong, that it bears full quotation:

> A series of welfare drives in large cities would, we believe, impel action on a new federal program to distribute income, eliminating the present public welfare system and alleviating the abject poverty which it perpetuates. Widespread campaigns to register the eligible poor for welfare aid, and to help existing recipients receive their full benefits, would produce bureaucratic disruption in welfare agencies and fiscal disruption in state

governments. These disruptions would generate severe political strains, and deepen existing divisions among elements in the big-city Democratic coalition: the remaining white middle class, the white working-class ethnic groups and the growing minority poor. To avoid a further weakening of that historic coalition, a national Democratic administration would be constrained to advance a federal solution to poverty that would override local welfare failures, local class and racial conflicts and local revenue dilemmas. By the internal disruption of local bureaucratic practices, by the furor over public welfare poverty, and by the collapse of current financing arrangements, powerful forces can be generated for major economic reforms at the national level.

The authors may deserve credit for thinking dialectically, but not for much else. Who could seriously believe—even in an era of prosperity and possibility—that the government would react to a "furor" precipitated by the poor with anything other than a crackdown? Who could think that putting more people on welfare, even if only "temporarily," was a good thing? It's not as if the idea that working is preferable to not working has been around only since Charles Murray. In 1964, reviewing a book on Appalachian poverty, W. Carey McWilliams, editor of the very journal in which the Piven and Cloward article had appeared, argued in *Dissent* that welfare "has become a dole, based on no sense of worth or contribution, accentuating the mountaineer's sense of weakness, depriving him of any sense of dignity." But Piven and Cloward's view was obviously quite a different one: in a 1967 *Nation* article, they actually described programs to find jobs for welfare recipients as "a serious threat to the movement." Finally, the authors' argument that dividing the middle class, the working class, and the poor would be a good thing was, of course, just the sort of disastrous cant for which the left is still paying a dear price (to say nothing of the poor people themselves).

Two of Piven and Cloward's goals were to enumerate for recipients precisely what benefits they had coming to them—often, caseworkers weren't forthcoming with such information—and to let people who were being denied aid know how they might in fact qualify. Nothing wrong with that. But their theory was completely unrealistic and probably dangerous. It did, however, have the unfortunate virtue of being half right. Between the mid-'60s and the early '70s, the welfare rolls in New York City doubled, from about 500,000 to a million (the number today is about 1.2 million). This happened for many reasons—the continuing flight from the cities of manufacturers and other low-skill employers, primarily—other than Piven and Cloward's campaign. The bottom line is that there was a crisis, all right, but somehow the American political leadership didn't respond quite so charitably as the authors had promised.

Perhaps Piven and Cloward forgot, among other things, that there were elections that the Republicans might, and did, win (although it must be said that Richard Nixon is the only modern president to have worked with any seriousness toward implementing a guaranteed family income, which he gave up on after it failed to pass the Senate in 1972). The explosion of the welfare rolls that occurred in New York was replicated all over the country and, ever since, the effect has been quite predictably the direct opposite of what Piven and Cloward anticipated: not only did the War on Poverty end, but AFDC benefit levels have dropped by around 45 percent. The village has indeed been destroyed, but not, alas, saved.

Suppose, instead, that in the mid- to late '60s, when public opinion leaned more toward the liberal left than the right and society was more willing to engage in such experiments, the left had spent its energy devising a humane scheme for transferring people from welfare into jobs programs? Money for such adventures would have been more readily available then, even with Vietnam. After all, wasn't the notion of work the very core of radical politics from its inception; what's a proletariat, after all? Karl Marx—no Charles Murray, he—called productive activity "the life of the species." And yet the chief goal of what was arguably the most influential left-wing poor people's movement of the last 30 years was to encourage people *not* to work. Disrupting the system sounded far more radical and thus more appealing, and of course was far easier than setting about the genuine hard work of devising a program.

There's no need here to go over developments since then in any great detail, for the simple reason that nothing has changed very dramatically. After the failure of the welfare rights movement, the left did generally come to the view that success was better measured by removing people from welfare than by putting them on it, so that at least was a positive step. Beyond that, leftist commentary on the welfare situation has been marked, as noted previously, by many critiques and few ideas.

Such ideas as have come forth are usually either wrongheaded or too general to affect the debate. For an example of the former, we can skip ahead a few years to the early 1980s— and with Reagan in office, things are getting serious now—to Piven and Barbara Ehrenreich writing that the left's welfare reform agenda "should begin, very simply, with the demand for higher levels of benefits." Sure; that had an excellent chance of seeing the light of day in the Reagan years. Since then, the left's arguments really haven't been about welfare in a direct sense. They've involved more encompassing demands for full employment, livable wages, and subsidized day care so that women can leave their children during the day. As these demands have gone nowhere in a conservative era, the left has placed more emphasis on critiquing the right's arguments and theses, trying to do two things: first, to erase the notion, advanced by conservatives over recent years in increasingly agitated fashion, that poor people, and especially the black poor, are poor primarily because of some moral or ethical deficiency of their own; and second, to prove that every proposed reform, whether advanced by conservatives or liberals, is reactionary, unworkable, or (preferably) both.

With the first goal I have little disagreement. I share the belief, and I can't imagine anyone on the left not sharing it, that most poor people are poor not because of their behavior but because of circumstances—economic dislocation, declining wages, unemployment and underemployment, and discrimination—that they can do little or nothing about. All these factors, of course, tend to hit minorities harder than whites. More white people, especially those who insist that they rose up by their own bootstraps and others should do the same, need to understand that the difficulties of blacks and Latinos have far more to do with the job market than with straps, boot or any other sort. When white Americans' forebears—my forebears—arrived from Italy, Ireland, Russia, wherever, the economy was bursting with blue-collar jobs that ill-educated people could fill easily, and diligent employees could find jobs for life; indeed, there were often jobs that their children could have for life as well. By the time blacks were permitted reasonable access to the labor market and Latino immigration began *en masse* (both started in the late '50s), there were far fewer blue-collar jobs, because of both economic dislocation and racism on the part of employers and trade unions. Whites would also do well to understand the extent to which, when urban neighborhoods "turned," landlords let their own buildings crumble and burn and banks refused to lend money. With respect to black people in particular, too few whites know or care at this point that slavery forced the separation of families and held it illegal for blacks to learn to read and write, and that under Jim Crow very few blacks could own anything or transact their own commerce (this is not merely ancient history; Martin Luther King, Jr., visited some Alabama sharecroppers as recently as 1965 and was shocked to learn that they'd never seen American currency). In the face of that history, black people on the whole have had to work much harder than others to get where they are today, and a less strong people might never have outlived the "peculiar" institution in the first place. Conservative accounts blaming black people for their poverty almost never consider any of these factors, or treat them as bygone and therefore irrelevant matters, and the left has done well to highlight these points.

Like most reporters, I've visited poor neighborhoods and interviewed poor people. The vast majority, of course, have fine "values." They work or want to work, they go to church, they join neighborhood groups and attend community meetings, and they try, against difficult odds, to give their children everything they can. When apartment buildings are full of exposed asbestos and wiring from the 1940s, and when elevators are so dangerous that children die falling down the shafts (this happens more often than nonurban readers might think), of whose values does such decrepitude speak—the tenants', or the owners' and inspectors'? When practically half the children in a neighborhood are asthmatic, as is the case in Mott Haven in the Bronx, whose values led to the befouled air that makes them sick? These conditions are not the result of the moral and ethical deficiencies of poor people, but of decision makers. The left has argued this for years, to sadly little avail, but it has been right to do so.

The second aspect of the left's critiques, however—denouncing all proposals as reactionary and impugning the integrity of those who make them—has been a huge problem. Virtually any proposal or attempt at reform is reflexively denounced as a fraud and a sham. The original, precollapse Clinton plan, giving recipients job training and two years to find work, was of course mocked on the left. Journalist Mickey Kaus proposed a massive public works program to shift people gradually from welfare to work. Instead of seeing what good there might be in the idea—and there are progressive aspects to it, even if it's again a little unrealistic to imagine today's government spending the billions such a program would require—the left's typical response was that it reinforces "the shame of the dole and the virtue of labor, no matter the job and no matter the pay" (Piven and Cloward again, 26 years later). It also helps to identify Kaus repeatedly as a "neoliberal," which flashes the signal to others on the left that Kaus probably consorts at cocktail parties with people like Moynihan and is thus not to be trusted (and he probably does, but so what?). Financier Felix Rohatyn has made similar proposals, less from the perspective of reforming welfare than of rebuilding the nation's infrastructure. There are arguments to be made against Rohatyn's proposal, particularly that the 25-cent-per-gallon gasoline tax he proposes to finance it would be murder on working people, but usually the plan is dismissed simply because it's Rohatyn's—he *is* an investment banker, after all, so he must have an ulterior motive. Jesse Jackson embraced it briefly but, as is his unfortunate wont, stopped after he'd squeezed as much press coverage out of it as he could.

Again, the point is not that leftist critiques of these proposals are all wrong. But it is undeniably the left's tendency to find what's wrong with others' ideas rather than what may be right with them, to impute bad motives to their proponents, or to take a line of text or one plank in a proposal as proof that the writer has moved to the right or the proposal is reactionary. The left has uniformly excoriated New Jersey's welfare overhaul, for example, which is best known for the "family cap" that denies welfare mothers higher benefits when they have additional children. But the fact is that the plan was not the evil creation of right-wing legislators from areas with few minorities and low welfare rates. The reform was led by Wayne Bryant, an African American Democratic state senator from Camden, one of the state's poorest cities. Bryant can hardly be accused of being uncaring. The plan he helped draw up does indeed eliminate increases in benefits for additional children, but it also does things that are less discussed: it permits a mother to marry without facing the automatic loss of benefits; it eliminates the standard 30 percent reduction in benefits when both parents live in the home; it provides child care services and tutoring; and it allows recipients who do get jobs to stay on Medicaid for two years rather than the federally mandated one year. In fact, Bryant points out, New Jersey is spending *more* money, not less, under this supposedly horrifying plan. The results, which Bryant laid out in an October 1995 *Washington Post* article, include a doubling of the number of AFDC recipients with jobs and a dramatic increase in education and job training programs. Also, though Bryant concedes that the figures are incomplete, the number of births has gone down.

Is there absolutely nothing in the New Jersey plan for the left to build on, absolutely nothing about it that's progressive? The plan plainly has some good, even generous, aspects. Admittedly, it's an amalgam of approaches from both left and right, and as such provides yet another example of the way in which those categories can hinder actual progress. The Washington, D.C., City Council, mostly black (and the whites are mostly liberal), passed a family cap like New Jersey's in its welfare bill: are these people right-wingers? No, they're just looking for answers. But the left cannot move beyond its slogans. Constructive thinking about exactly how the current welfare system rewards and punishes recipients and what's wrong with it is time-consuming and not very popular. What's easy, and what gets people's attention, is isolating one plank out of several as proof that a plan is racist and sexist—identity politics at work again—and that it's just a different set of walls around the same prison.

But by sitting out the debate, by gesturing from the sidelines, the left is helping to maintain the prison. Because while the left has been busy issuing its critiques, the right has been issuing ideas in a mad torrent. Thus, the conservatives lead the dialogue; moderates and liberals follow, fine-tuning conservative proposals to make them less harsh and occasionally producing ideas of their own; and the left watches from the bleachers, failing to match either right or center with ideas of its own and refusing to talk about the welfare problem in any but macroeconomic terms. And those are not terms that have any hope of getting through to the mass of people. In a self-fulfilling downward spiral, the left's failure to offer concrete alternatives clears the field for the right and the center to present their programs to the broader public. And when people latch onto those programs—as they inevitably do, since the left presents no alternatives—the left writes them off as reactionaries.

The left doesn't engage in these debates, because to be radical is to refuse to accept the stated premises of the argument. Fair enough; a radical critique of poverty in this country will always focus less on poverty programs per se, which are mostly tepid and mildly ameliorative, than on the larger context in which the richest nation on Earth permits such ghastly conditions to persist. Such a critique holds that poverty and the welfare system need not exist at all, and wouldn't if only 1 percent of the population didn't own 40 percent of the wealth, if only workers had some say in the running of corporations and businesses, if only a few billion—AFDC costs roughly $15 billion a year—were taken from the Pentagon's annual budget of about $240 billion, if only the government attacked the billions in corporate subsidies and tax shelters, and so on. Clearly, these points makes sense. And attacking corporate

welfare and Pentagon profligacy, and pushing for wage increases and subsidized day care programs must be central to a
program that seeks to ally the middle and working classes with
the poor and to redirect money toward the social needs of all
people.

But exhortation needs a program behind it. Marshalling
those arguments makes leftists nod their heads in agreement
and pat themselves and one another on the back for having
the correct analysis. But then what? Those arguments don't
constitute an adequate response to the current debate. And
the truth is that something is deeply wrong with the welfare
system, irrespective of whether the United States spends $240
billion on the Pentagon or half that, and regardless of whether
the minimum wage is $4.25 or $10.50 an hour. Even though
90 percent of conservative rhetoric about the behavioral problems of poor people is both mendacious and mean, three
things are true: first and foremost, working must be honored
above not working, because it is essential to human dignity
and even to liberty; second, welfare has created miserable de-
pendence among those stuck in its maw; and third, those most
stuck tend to be teenage mothers who are bearing children
they can't support (and the men fathering these children are
unwilling or unable to support them).

Even if, as Piven and Ehrenreich and others have suggested, benefit levels were high enough to place recipients
above the poverty line—even if they totalled, say, $30,000 a
year—would that be a good thing? Given the left's history on
the topic—the fact that probably its major contribution has
been to expand the rolls—many on the left would probably say
that it *would* be a good thing. But it's nonsense. As Betsy Reed
pointed out in an article in *Dollars & Sense*, "lifting people out
of poverty through work is still the method most women on
welfare say they would prefer." As far as I'm concerned, those
women are the experts, and I'll take their word for it. Reed, in

a thoughtful article from 1994, criticizes workfare programs such as those profferred by Clinton and Massachusetts Governor William Weld as expensive and inadequate, but she also found several programs around the country that were doing a decent job of moving poor women into jobs, such as the GAIN program in California. It certainly has problems, Reed writes, but overall it "offers real but incremental improvements over the welfare status quo." That "incremental" sounds dour but let's face it, dramatic changes for the better, in any context, are hard to come by.

There are other such programs around the country. Robin Epstein, writing in *In These Times* (the only left-wing journal, to my reading, that consistently publishes welfare-related stories that go beyond the usual chatter about what frauds and shams the reforms are), located a group in Milwaukee called Congress for a Working America. Its program, Project Hope, succeeded in Epstein's eyes precisely because it refuses to draw firm ideological lines. It provides health care and child care, which the left supports, but it also places people in community service jobs—when other alternatives are lacking—which the left usually doesn't approve of because they're not career-path jobs.

Articles like Reed's and Epstein's at least try to look for positive existing models across the country, rather than just pointing the usual fingers at the usual suspects. They also implicitly recognize that solving a problem in the real world, especially one as desperately intractable as welfare, is not something that can be accomplished through doctrine. Obviously, permanent jobs at a livable wage are preferable, but in some cases, a job flipping burgers for a brief time might help. The vast majority of Americans have performed such jobs at some point in their lives; they will always say, If it's good enough for me . . . , and they have a point. Progressives in New York City are dead set against a policy of Rudy Giuliani's to make able-bodied men without children who receive home relief perform public service work in the city's parks and other venues, but why is that inherently awful? Because it renders people into mere chattel of the state? That's posturing. In real life, for some people on home relief, it just might work out and lead to a job with the Parks Department or the transit authority.

Left and right are both guilty of applying inflexible ideology to a real world in which the factors in operation are far more complicated and nuanced than either side allows. The right fails the poor for obvious reasons: its belief that the unfettered market can take care of everyone, which it can't, and its political attacks on welfare recipients, especially those who are black and female. But the left is failing them, too. By concentrating its efforts on defending welfare mothers against conservative attacks and by refusing to get involved in the welfare reform debate with real, specific ideas, the left has ensured that no one listens or takes it seriously. The tragedy of its failure is that poor people, of course, are desperate for someone truly to grasp and come to terms with the problems of poverty, especially the urban poverty from which there really seems to be no escape for so many people of color.

That desperation was expressed by Laura Matthews, a social worker in Illinois, whom Chicago journalist Salim Muwakkil interviewed for *In These Times* in early 1995. Muwakkil wrote that Matthews, who works in Chicago's notorious Robert Taylor Homes, "has witnessed the effects of the system from a ringside seat" and is "more convinced than Newt Gingrich that it has supplied a knock-out punch to the African-American family" (can you imagine any left-wing intellectual or spokesperson acknowledging that?). Matthews knows, too, that real jobs at good wages are the ultimate answer, and her work is to do what she can to move women into those jobs and help them perform them well. But in Muwakkil's article she voices desperate frustration with both the status quo and the lack of ideas for changing it, saying at one point: "In some ways I applaud Newt Gingrich and the Republicans. I figure we need a major shake-up and their strategy may be just what we need. But then I think about the millions of people who will be hurt, and I come to my senses."

She and her clients are among the many people the left has let down with its defensiveness and lack of creativity. The left is paying the political price for this, and it's a steep one. But Matthews' clients are paying a price that's far higher.

Chapter 5

DOING THE RIGHT'S WORK

Immigration

Back in 1986, the southern California communities of Encinitas, Leucadia, Olivenhain, and Cardiff-by-the-Sea,
hoping to free themselves from the pro-growth mantra that
guided the San Diego County Board of Supervisors, got together and incorporated themselves into the city of Encinitas.
The incorporation gave the city the legal power to oppose the
county's growth policies and to protect the type of enclave
idealized by Hollywood's image factory—beachfront proper-
ties, nice homes with solid resale value, robust and accessible
commercial strips, the sort of place where the whirr of the
lawnmower and the soft buzz of the child's bicycle indicate a
lifestyle and pace not often interrupted by the world's various
crudenesses.

But this was southern California in the 1980s. So when the
new City Council met for the first time, the issue of newly
arrived immigrants living in lean-tos on public and private

118

property and gathering on street corners during the day to solicit work was waiting for the new legislators. The issue gave the city "a sense of being born into a crisis," as the *Los Angeles Times* described it: "At meetings that went long into the night, residents complained to the fledgling council of trash heaps, public urination and crime problems." The sides formed quickly, and the pattern of debate that ensued is one that's all too familiar today. After months of white-hot argument, a compromise was struck that would have fixed sanctions on employers who knowingly hired illegal immigrants—a federal law passed the same year imposed such sanctions as well—and required the city to operate a hiring hall for documented immigrants to ensure they were treated fairly. In the end, the American Civil Liberties Union and the California Rural League Assistance sued successfully to overturn the ordinance and ever since, Encinitans have lived with the *status quo ante*. And even though Marjorie Gaines, a city councilwoman who had been a vocal crackdown proponent, was defeated for reelection during the controversy, Encinitas was pointing the way in 1986 toward a fight that, eight years later, would consume California and that consumes the nation today.

The use of the word "nation," as opposed to "country" or some other loose designation, is deliberate. For immigration, like no other issue, forces everyone who gives the matter some thought to consider the United States not as a polity or a system of governance but *as a nation*—that is, as a nation of people with a national identity, culture, and character. As discussed in Chapter Three, the ideal of a universal American character is one that has been hymned since the country's beginnings. Indeed, it's often been said and is generally accepted that to be American is not to be of a certain stock or race or denomination, but to be committed to certain ideals—democracy, liberty, self-government—that, subverted as they often are in the name of national security and other such shrouds, are nevertheless the Constitution's finest expressions. As nationhoods go, this is one of the least demanding on the planet, requiring, for example, no allegiance to a church or a monarch or a dictator as so many nations do. As also detailed in Chapter Three, today's left regards this sort of rhetoric with suspicion; not without ample historical reason but, as I have argued, much to its detriment.

How one answers the immigration question says quite a lot about what sort of nation one conceives America to be. And how the government has treated the subject tells us the same. Until the harsh Johnson-Reed immigration control laws of 1924, the people and their elected representatives had conceived of an ample, generous, highly differentiated, and heterogeneous nation, notable exceptions such as the Chinese Exclusion Act of 1882 notwithstanding. The years 1880 to 1920 marked, of course, the great immigrant wave of Italians, Jews, Russians, Slavs, Poles, and others (the Irish had already been coming, as had other northern Europeans, many before there were any immigration laws at all). In fact, 23.5 million came in those years, and in the 1910s, foreign-born people accounted for nearly 15 percent of the total U.S. population, the highest percentage ever. The famous phrase "the melting pot" was coined then, in a 1908 play by Israel Zangwill in which the lead characters were a Russian couple who could never have married in the old country, owing to proscriptions of blood and class, but who do so in New York. The massive influx was, we all agree now, one of the great triumphs of our history.

But at the time, it led to some ghastly bigotry directed at southern and eastern Europeans that was precisely the sort one sometimes hears today directed at new immigrants (uneducated, ill-read, pestilent, etc.) and, finally, to the infamous clampdown of 1924, when strict quotas by country were set (by a Republican Congress and White House). Those quotas were higher for European nations than others, the justification being that immigration should be based on a person's, and a people's, historic links to the United States, and were implemented with the clear intent of keeping out the darker hued. For the next 60 years, few were allowed in at all, with minor exceptions like postwar legislation that brought some displaced persons to America and the *bracero* program that brought in some Mexicans to work during the war (in the early '50s, they were deported). The 1952 McCarran-Walter Act eliminated the racial barriers of the 1924 act with regard to Asians, but numerical quotas were still tight, with the effect that nothing much changed. Two statistics show the (intentional) impact of McCarran-Walter: in the '50s, only 2.5 million immigrants came to the United States overall, a trickle compared to the peak decades; and from 1952 to 1965, only 61 percent of all available visas were used, because many of those who wanted to come were from the "wrong" countries.

It was the Immigration Act of 1965 that set today's current patterns, and if the civil rights laws are taken collectively as Lyndon Johnson's finest hour, the Immigration Act is surely an underrated second, even if its purpose wasn't as magnanimous as its results suggest. Signed (where else?) at the Statue of Liberty in October of that year, the act sought to correct the racist history of U.S. immigration law. It greatly liberalized numerical quotas, setting broad hemispheric targets and raising the worldwide total to 290,000 annually. It eliminated criteria based on race or historical links to America. Further, family reunification was instituted as a goal, so naturalized citizens could bring in members of their immediate family and, crucially, these entrants were not counted against the newly set quotas. It did impose, for the first time, a quota on immigration from the Western Hemisphere, which created a backlog at the beginning, but the family reunification strategy and other aspects of the act more than outweighed this.

The scholar Nicolaus Mills, among others, has noted that the act's supporters "did not believe it would substantially change immigration numbers." But guess what? By the 1970s, immigration had doubled over pre-act levels; by the '80s, it had increased even further, very nearly to the levels seen before 1924. In this decade, after the passage of another immigration law in 1990 that had the net effect of keeping most tenets of the '65 act in place and increasing the numbers, legal immigration to the United States has risen to levels that are practically an all-time high: an average of 1.2 million people a year from 1990 through 1993, the last year for which full figures were available at the time of this writing. If immigration, as I stated above, is a yardstick by which we measure what kind of a nation we are, it must be said that since 1965, and especially over the past 15 or so years, we've a record of generosity to be proud of.

Looking at the patterns of newcomers by country of origin should reinforce this pride. One hears and reads a lot from today's left about what an incorrigibly racist and xenophobic country the United States is—a subject I'll return to in more detail later—and that's undoubtedly true of much right-wing rhetoric, particularly about illegal immigrants. But as far as official policy is concerned, the opposite is emphatically the case. In fact, U.S. immigration policy is probably the single *least* racist aspect of this country's political life. Consider: from 1989 to 1993 inclusive, according to Immigration and Naturalization Service figures, 2.375 million people came to the United States legally from Mexico, the Third World country with the highest total, while from Russia, the European country with the highest total, we've taken in just 147,000 people. We've taken in more Jamaicans than Britons, far more Haitians than French, more from a few small countries in the Caribbean and Central America than from the whole of Europe, and more than two-and-a-half times as many Asians as Europeans. All told, about 80 percent of all immigrants in the last five years have arrived from what could be called "countries of color," with the other 20 percent coming from Europe and Canada. And the European numbers are probably higher than they might be because of communism's collapse, which opened the doors to Eastern bloc emigration. Admittedly, African migration numbers are low, not because any policies against immigration from those countries exist—they don't—but because emigration from Africa tends more toward Europe than the United States and because emigration from the poorest countries of the world, many of which are on that continent, is typically a trickle (except when the country is proximal, as in Haiti's case). But overall, the influx has been astonishing.

Of course, anyone living in or near a large city or in the handful of states that have absorbed the bulk of these arrivals (California, New York, Texas, Florida, Illinois, New Jersey) knows intuitively what these numbers say. And what the numbers translate into, in people's real lives, is exactly what the United States should be about at its core. People absorb American customs and bring us theirs: a constant interchange of cause and effect by which, in the old days, Italian and Slavic traditions, and today, Caribbean and Filipino ones, become American, while American traditions are taken up by those groups. New as today's immigration patterns are, we cannot yet see fully the contributions these immigrants will make to the language, to science, to the arts and literature, to our customs, to our demotic whole; but over time, those contributions will become apparent. The virtually endless elasticity of American culture is probably the single best thing about this country; it is multiculturalism in its true and good sense—not the faux-radical multiculturalism found in slogans chanted on college campuses about "Western culture" having to "go"—and these days, blessedly, there is scarcely an area of the country immune from its effects. Indeed, though these effects are more apparent in cities, one need not live in New York or Los Angeles to have felt the impact already. My hometown, population about 40,000 and tucked away in Appalachia, didn't have a pizza parlor until the 1960s or a Chinese restaurant until the '70s, about the same time it got its first McDonald's. Today, there is a reasonably impressive array of options for the curious eater, with pockets of diverse population to match, in a place where life is comparatively easy and people get along pretty well (and still don't vote Republican).

The example of my hometown may seem too narrowly focused, but restaurants and other forms of entrepreneurship are precisely the way to measure what many see as the greatest contribution of immigrants—namely, what they put into the economy. And study after study has shown that legal immigrants contribute far more in productivity than they consume in services and that the immigrant work force, on average, is hungry for success and, in fact, more productive than the native-born. This stands to reason, because immigrants of whatever decade and whatever color work terribly hard, often at jobs that other Americans don't want to do. Some conservatives who want to restrict immigration quote studies showing that immigrants are a drain on public services as a whole, but by such measures, we all are. People who were born here use parks, public transportation, interstate highways, and other public benefices; and after all, immigrants pay taxes too.

Of course, this massive level of immigration has not been without its problems. First, there are tensions, mostly generational, within the immigrant groups themselves: invariably—and this was as true of Poles and Italians in the past as it is of Koreans and Dominicans today—the children of fresh immigrants want to assimilate, while their children, the third generation, tend to reject assimilation to some extent and emphasize their native identity. Second, there are tensions

between the new immigrant groups and the country's established minorities, particularly black Americans. Black Americans' experience with this country's power elite is unique, and
immigrants of color, even those who are black, often don't face
the discrimination that black Americans have faced and find it
easier to make their way here. Finally, of course, there are tensions between the immigrant groups and the white majority.

The two latter categories of tensions are at bottom over
jobs—specifically, the sense of native-born blacks and whites
that immigrants are taking jobs that they should be filling.
There is something to their suspicion, and this is the point
where our liberal and enlightened immigration laws are, in
one respect, perhaps not so liberal and enlightened after all. It
was not for nothing that the immigration law of 1990, which
increased immigration levels, received the backing of 41
Senate Republicans and the signature of a Republican president. Many on the right have supported a generous immigration policy precisely because immigrants provide a willing and
more easily exploitable labor force. As the writer Michael Lind
has put it: "A generous immigration policy, resulting in a
constant supply of unskilled, poor immigrants, competing
with poor and less-educated Americans for a fixed supply of
jobs, has the same effect as the enlargement of the labor pool
through the expatriation of American-owned industry. It
keeps wages low and unions weak—to the benefit of the white
overclass."

Thus has *The Wall Street Journal* editorialized in favor of an
open borders policy, while many labor unions have taken the
seemingly conservative position of wanting to slow the flow.
Other conservative organs, such as the business magazines,
are less expansive than the *Journal* but nevertheless want immigration kept at high levels. So it's apparent that the Peter
Brimelow school of cultural conservatism—he of the book
that openly argued for keeping America as white and Anglo-

Saxon as possible—is at odds with corporate conservatism, which wants the cheap hands. There is little question but that immigrants, particularly poorly educated and unskilled ones—and the standards immigrants must meet to be permitted entry are not high—are of great benefit to big business and to rich people in general, whom they often serve as maids and nannies, and are actually something of a bane to working-class people already here (not through any active fault of their own, of course, but simply because their presence, as Lind says, helps keep wages low and unions weak). And, as Lind also noted, free trade agreements such as NAFTA, which do not include built-in assurances of the right to unionize and other codicils that might help drive wages up in countries like Mexico (instead of driving them down here, which NAFTA is doing), have much the same effect.

The dilemma of wanting to welcome new people and their immense contributions on the one hand, and needing to create (and not preserve, since wages are declining in real terms) a living wage structure on the other, is the challenge of developing a coherent progressive immigration policy.

But dealing with legal immigration is comparatively easy. Americans have generally supported fairly high levels of legal immigration in recent years, although cutting back has popular support in the polls today and will probably happen in the near future. But the bigger and nastier issue is that of illegal immigration—the 300,000 to 400,000 people a year who have no papers, who come here either by literally jumping or cutting through the fence between the United States and Mexico or by paying an exorbitant fee for passage from China and other points, and who work for slave wages in death-trap environments.

The situation of illegals is the subject of especially intense debate. Although the right is split on this question, as it is on legal immigration, between the cultural conservatives who want restrictions and the big businesses, especially agribusinesses, that want the cheap labor, the restrictionists tend to win the day when it comes to illegals. The reasons are simple enough: illegal immigrants are perceived as not having played by the rules and, compared to legal immigrants, they are somewhat more likely to cost the economy more than they contribute. Although illegal aliens are not entitled to certain public services to which legals are entitled, court decisions over the years have outlawed denying some services to illegal immigrants and especially to their children. The 1982 Supreme Court ruling in *Plyer v. Doe*, for example, held that children of illegal immigrants are entitled to a free public education. Besides, the tangible, concrete border through which illegals sneak makes a lively and useful symbol for the right, as do those murky videoclips we've all seen of a man cutting a hole in the fence and six or eight or more people racing through.

And so a minor cottage industry of anti-immigrant organizations has sprung up on the nativist right: the Federation for American Immigration Reform is probably the best known, because of its involvement in California's Proposition 187 and because of the presence within its orbit of Alan C. Nelson, who headed the INS under George Bush. FAIR, interestingly enough, has environmentalist ties as well, and its anti-immigrant position tends to be based more on quasi-Malthusian arguments about population control than on fears that the cultural well is being poisoned. The American Immigration Control Foundation traffics more in cultural arguments, warning of riots and the like if immigration isn't controlled. There are conservative lawmakers—a few in Congress, more in state legislatures—who have alighted on immigration restriction as a winner of an issue. And of course there are the national spokespersons—Brimelow, mentioned above, and Pat Buchanan—who whip up xenophobia. Behind all the thunder and sometimes quite ugly rhetoric, their positions usually boil down to two: control the border more tightly (the U.S.- Mexico border is 2,000 miles long, but only 250 miles of that is traversable and most people come in through three or four main entry points), and end welfare and other public payments to illegals.

To which the left responds with . . . Well, that's the problem. Anything that can reasonably be called a left-wing position on what to do about immigration has yet to present itself. The view, such as it is, comes down to this: attacks on illegals are racist scapegoating. A 1992 article in Z *Magazine* called "Blaming the Newcomers," which runs to about 4,000 words, documents right-wing flourishes against immigration but makes no suggestion that illegal immigration might be a legitimate concern (indeed, the word illegal is placed within those quotation marks that are meant to convey haughty irony). A 1993 *Nation* article, headlined "The Scapegoats," analyzes "nativist paranoia" against Arab immigrants in the wake of the World Trade Center bombings, and a 1994 article from the same magazine highlights "Five Myths About Immigration," the conclusion of which is that if we are judged by how we treat others, "we are not in very good shape" (no mention, of course, of the fact that immigration is at its highest level since 1920). A *Progressive* commentary from 1993 attacks "racist and alarmist" articles from the news media— actually, it doesn't specifically cite any—and seeks to demonstrate that the very notion of controlling the border is racist and xenophobic. Indeed, a Border Patrol operation on the El Paso–Juarez border in 1993 was roundly rebuked in the left press for the usual reasons. An issue of the journal *Crossroads* largely devoted to the topic says little more than the others; an article headed "Scapegoating Without Boarders" decries the "bigoted fear and violence" that are "the order of the day" and avers that the U.S. Border Patrol is the "worst expression of institutionalized anti-immigrant violence and hysteria." The novelist Leslie Marmon Silko writes in *The Nation* about driving late at night through New Mexico and being stopped by Border Patrol cops, observing that a "police state" has developed in the American Southwest and concluding that borders are of "no use."

Like its critiques of right-wing positions on welfare, some of the left's charges have merit; without question, racism and xenophobia are inherent in the nativist right's anti-immigrant crusades. More importantly, when native-born Americans— white, black, Asian, and Latino—blame their economic insecurity on immigration rather than on the real culprit—the corporations and rich people whose share of the tax burden has declined so drastically in the last 20 years—that's wrong and must be pointed out. But as with welfare, to make these points is not to lay out a position, except, perhaps, the implicit position that borders are an imperialistic construct that should be done away with and that illegals should be given all due rights and be entitled to everything. That sounds nice on paper and has the added virtue of being impervious to accusations of racism, but it's completely unrealistic and, it can well be argued, not terribly progressive at all. It is, after all, exactly what many sectors of corporate America and their press agents on *The Wall Street Journal*'s editorial page want, it's exactly what the sleaze captains who operate disgusting sweatshops want, and it is exactly what rich people, who use illegals to rear their children and plant their impatiens, want. Thus do the left wing of multicultural identity, to which the word "illegal" is somehow expressive of false consciousness, and the right wing of capitalist economics, which wants exploitable hands, link arms and become one.

There is, to put it bluntly, an overwhelming unwillingess to deal with the issue. This was caught well by Ruben Navarette, Jr., in a column he wrote in the *Los Angeles Times* in March

1994. Surveying the nasty landscape, which included a beastly piece of federal legislation by California's Dana Rohrabacher targeting the children of illegals in public schools, Navarette wondered where the Congressional Hispanic Caucus stood on immigration. The answer?

> Mostly in hiding. On the caucus agenda for this Congress, immigration is buried at No. 7. When the subject is mentioned, it is only with regard to monitoring enforcement of immigration laws to ensure that Latinos are not discriminated against. Nothing about deporting illegal immigrants from U.S. jails. Nothing about securing or revoking the citizenship birthright to the children of illegal immigrants. Nothing about safeguarding or eliminating education, health and welfare benefits for illegal immigrants. Nothing.

As I've argued in previous chapters, a collection of Democratic members of Congress is not the same thing as the left, but on this issue, the views of the Hispanic Caucus are essentially those of the majority of the left. Can you imagine, a group of Latino lawmakers—in the year of Proposition 187, in the year that found foul legislation such as Rohrabacher's in the hopper, in the year that a major presidential commission was formed to recommend new immigration strategies—ranking immigration as only the seventh most important issue facing the land? The caucus, like much of the left, is deeply concerned with the employer sanctions section of the 1986 Immigration Reform and Control Act. That act permitted illegals who'd arrived before 1982 to apply for citizenship, but eliminated the possibility of naturalization for those who'd arrived after. It also imposed sanctions on employers whom inspectors found to have knowingly hired illegals, which has led to discrimination against legal immigrants who "look like" they may be illegal (documents are easy to forge, inspection is minimal). Sanctions have neither stemmed illegal immigration, as its authors hoped, nor proven a very enlightened means of enforcement, to say the least. But sanctions are not at the center of the problem.

Navarette points out the difficult truth of the matter, which is that national polls "invariably find Latinos more eager than the rest of the population to control the nation's borders." In other words, Latinos, like many other Americans, recognize illegal immigration as a problem, but the Hispanic Caucus cannot bring itself to acknowledge that a problem exists, in the name of . . .Well, in the name of what? In the name of fighting racism? So the 70-plus percent of Latinos (and within that, the 75 percent of Mexican Americans) Navarette refers to in his column who want tighter border controls are racist toward Mexicans? There is an attitude shift among immigrant groups, which occurred among Europeans earlier in the century and occurs today, known colloquially as "shutting the door behind them." Undoubtedly, that's at work here. It is also true that some portion of these Latinos are conservative (Cuban Americans tend toward the right). But most Latinos who vote are Democrats, and if they can be expected to be liberal on any issue, surely it is the question of the immigration rights of their brothers and sisters. So it just may be that they're not racists or right-wingers, but that they recognize a legitimate issue of concern.

No one should be fooled into thinking that massive border patrols are the only answer. Illegal immigration is a result of global economic shifts that, as Richard Rothstein observed in an intelligent discussion of the issue in *Dissent*, cannot "be reversed by more vigilant policing." But the general drift of leftist writing on the topic is not merely that full border control is unrealizable, but that it is undesirable. All the warnings about racism and police states have the effect of stopping the conversation, because once you've decided that the problem lies with the corrupt power structure and that race is at the root,

you really don't have to say anything else. This rhetoric is delivered, let's recall, in the context of an official immigration
policy that has delivered to these shores more than 15 million
people of color, from Asia, Latin America, and Africa, in the
last 15 years. That's one-fifth of all immigration to America
since records began to be kept in 1820. One is inclined toward
the unfortunate conclusion that left-wing analysis of the problem is not simply inadequate but dead wrong.

The insufficiency and wrongheadedness of the left's arguments reached their tragic nadir with the passage of Proposition 187 in California in 1994. I hold no brief whatsoever for
that terrible document, which seeks to bar illegal immigrants
from receiving all but the most basic public services (like
emergency medical treatment). Critics were right to point out
that it's utterly unworkable, first because most service providers are decent people whose commitment to their professions
will not permit them to turn the sick or the poor away, and
second because you can't have children born in this country
and refuse to educate them. That's immoral. Various remarks
of the proposition's sponsors suggest that they know it's not
practicable and are really seeking court tests to overturn the
aforementioned *Plyer v. Doe* and other decisions that give illegals and their children the right to public services. Harold
Ezell, one of its co-authors, said this outright in the weeks
leading up to the vote.

Nevertheless, Prop 187 passed with 59 percent of the vote.
And it passed with the support of some 40 to 50 percent of
black and Asian voters and 20 to 25 percent of Latino voters.
Why? Because, again, the left's arguments against it were not
compelling to enough people outside the movements that
made up the opposition. The best the opposition could do was
to issue the expedient acknowledgement that illegal immigration is a problem—an acknowledgement, as we've seen, that

the left doesn't really believe should be made—but that this measure was not the answer. And it never quite said what the answer was. This was the moderate wing of the opposition talking, a coalition funded by business groups and P.T.A.s that hired a conservative public relations firm to get the message out—probably a foolish move since the firm was best known for its ballot work on behalf of huge corporate clients. Frustrated with that tack, the more grassroots opponents of Prop 187 split off into another organization that attacked it primarily on the standard grounds of racism and xenophobia, and by means of scare tactics: 400,000 children will be thrown out on the streets, California will lose billions in federal funds, and so on. An organizer of the grassroots group who criticized the establishment group's willingness to recognize illegal immigration as a legitimate issue was quoted in *The Nation* as saying that "even if Proposition 187 is defeated, the use of these kinds of arguments will be detrimental to all of us afterwards." Needless to say, counterarguments were not offered up.

The question comes down to this: without a doubt, many racist and xenophobic people and organizations supported Prop 187; but is everyone who votes for such a measure a racist or a xenophobe? Absolutely not. In late September of '94, a *Los Angeles Times* reporter spoke with a Latina woman—a tax examiner who had once worked on a Central Valley farm—who said: "I have a heart. I am human. But each time I walk out my door, I think, 'Oh, boy. Something has got to be done about this problem.'" In the same article, a self-described "very liberal" woman who ran a theater troupe planned to vote in favor of 187: "Entering the country illegally by definition is breaking the law. To reward people for that with health and public education is just ethically wrong . . . The law has to mean something." The history of radical activism shows that many laws need breaking, of course, but a law as racially liberal as American immigration law does not necessarily rank among them.

The left completely misread this, as a left so transfixed with identity was bound to. And as the ethnic and racial breakdown of the results shows, appeals to racial solidarity are not enough for most people of color (who are multifaceted, live complicated lives, etc.), and appeals based on racial guilt aren't compelling to very many white people anymore. This does not make them racists; it means that they, too, have complicated lives and complicated problems that slogans can't address. Admittedly, it does mean that they are susceptible to a frenzy of foreign-bashing, but when given a choice between something awful (Prop 187) and nothing (the left's alternative), people are going to opt for something awful, and they can't really be blamed. The sight of Prop 187 opponents wearing buttons that said "I'm an illegal alien" and waving Mexican, rather than American, flags didn't help matters. During at least one anti-187 rally, several American flags were burned—a reflexively dumb act at best, and to the vast majority an odious one.

The misguided thinking continued after the vote. Several groups that had opposed Proposition 187 got together in December and announced a boycott of RJR Nabisco and Disney—the park, the films, all manner of Disney-iana, everything. Not because these corporations, whatever else one might have to say about them, were major backers of 187. They were not; they stayed neutral. But they had made contributions to Governor Pete Wilson and, since Wilson was so bound up with Prop 187, RJR and Disney were also culpable. This despite the fact that Disney had also donated money to Wilson's gubernatorial opponent, Democrat Kathleen Brown, who'd opposed 187! Naturally, it had to be thrown in for good measure that it had been discovered upon reinspection that portrayals of nonwhite peoples, and one supposes animals, in Disney cartoons had been found to promote stereotypes. Fortunately, cooler heads prevailed; *Los Angeles Times* columnist

George Ramos wrote that the boycott was "based on mis-
placed emotion" and "guilt by association," and other Latino
groups interceded.

In the previous chapter, I asked how the course of American
welfare policy might have been different had the left, rather
than demanding the expansion of welfare rights in the 1960s,
demanded a program centered on moving welfare recipients
off the dole and into work. Similarly, I wonder how different
today's immigration debate might look had the left been able
to accept that illegal immigration is a problem that transcends
racial and ethnic categories and offered ways to address it hu-
manely. Now, of course, with the left's refusal to do so, the
issue is being addressed by the right, on the right's terms, with
potentially disastrous results for illegal immigrants and their
children.

One doubts, further, that it will stop there. The generous
levels of immigration this country has permitted in recent
years should be applauded by liberals and leftists, but another
set of people look at those numbers and come away with an
altogether different interpretation. A reaction against legal
immigration is under way now, with proposals by some conservatives in Congress that welfare benefits to legal immigrants
be reduced or even eliminated. The left could have done
something to try to avert this reaction by making a distinction
between legal and illegal immigration, arguing in defense of
the former and constructing a tenable position on the latter.
Its failure to do so is now placing legal immigration in
jeopardy, because many people have the sense that immigration—and most don't distinguish between legal and illegal—is
way out of control, and they sure don't have the sense that the
left has any answers. Joel Kotkin, in an insightful op-ed piece
in *The New York Times* a week before the vote, bemoaned the
opposition's refusal to see illegal immigration as an issue (he

quotes an anti-187 slogan: "No human being is illegal") and concluded that "until those who favor immigration face up to the storm over illegal entrants, this latest California tidal wave could end up extinguishing" legal immigration.

It also jeopardizes the refugee and asylum system, the third leg of immigration. The asylum system is replete with inconsistencies that stem from fossilized Cold War thinking. The most jarring recent example was that of desperate Haitians on jerry-built boats being refused entry into the United States, no doubt partly for racial reasons but also because this country's friendly relations with the deposed Duvalier regime had precluded any official acknowledgment that Haitians could face political repression at home. After Prop 187, the possibility that such policies can be made more humane seems unlikely.

Two weeks after Prop 187 passed, Robert Scheer wrote an op-ed piece in the *Los Angeles Times* that *did* present an idea, a new way of looking at the problem. The state of California, Scheer writes, "has long had the authority . . . to ensure that everyone who works is covered by workers' compensation and paid the minimum wage as well as time and a half for overtime and that accurate records, including tax deductions and proof of legal right to work, are maintained. Additionally, working conditions must meet Cal-OSHA standards as well as local health and fire-safety rules." That is to say, practically everything that makes it possible for U.S. employers to exploit illegals' labor is *already against the law*, as is, in many cases, the act of hiring illegals itself. So why do the practices continue? Because, as Scheer notes, "for the entire state, on a good day, there are only 16 inspectors to enforce the labor laws." Imagine how different things would be if the left had devoted all the time and energy it spent crying racism to lobbying for a three-fold or fourfold increase in the number of labor inspectors. The unlawful exploitation by employers of illegal immigrants might have abated and the general problem eased somewhat. At the very least, such a strategy would have done more actual good for illegal immigrants than has been accomplished by the incessant invocations of racism.

Of course, illegals come here not because of U.S. working conditions primarily, but because of working conditions at home (which is, in most cases, Mexico). Obviously, improved conditions and wages there is the only real long-term solution, and Rothstein and others on the left have made this point effectively, as have some congressional Democrats. But that will take years, if it happens at all; it will require profound changes in the NAFTA and GATT accords, for starters, that will be extremely difficult to achieve in a climate in which those documents have bipartisan support.

In the meantime, it's not unreasonable to acknowledge that something should be done. Denying benefits is crude and lacking in compassion. But there are other possible answers. Sadly, the most thorough piece of anti-Prop 187 agitprop I have found came not from the left but from William Bennett and Jack Kemp, two leading conservatives who famously opposed the initiative. In the *Wall Street Journal* op-ed piece in which they laid out their position, Bennett and Kemp analyzed the problem, explained their opposition, and then went on to do something left-wing journalism almost never does: they listed seven points that amounted to an alternative strategy. Some of these are ideas the left would not and should not sign on to (expand NAFTA), but others are not unreasonable (step up border patrols, crack down on fraudulent documents, speed up the deportation of illegals convicted of a crime). Of course, today's left would consider it racist to think about even those steps, which leaves nowhere to turn.

The left is not going to win this debate by accusing people who express legitimate concern of prejudice and leaving it at

that. Screaming *j'accuse* is not a program. Nor is it a vision of
what the American nation should be.

Or perhaps it is a vision, but it's not a salutary one. It's a
vision in which citizenship counts for nothing. If no one is illegal, as the anti-187 slogan suggested, it follows that no one is
legal. The blurring of such distinctions, and the concomitant
disruption of a seemingly conservative notion like national integrity, seems to sound radical to a lot of people. But consider
the implications. To be a legal citizen, whether native-born or
naturalized, is to possess rights that cannot be violated by the
state. Those rights can be put to use both privately and publicly: to live as one pleases, to worship (or not) as one pleases,
to say what one pleases, to divorce oneself from the country's
affairs if one chooses or to try to change the country for the
better. Citizens may no longer control their lucre-infested and
all too undemocratic government, if indeed they ever did, but
at least the government cannot control them. Citizenship, in
other words, is the individual's shield against the intrusions of
the state. But to expand citizenship to infinitude, as many on
the left apparently want, to erase U.S. citizenship as a category
that has legitimacy, is to make it lose its meaning. When citizenship ceases to have meaning, the shield is forfeited; the
state can do anything it pleases and eventually, people become
not citizens but subjects.

I can't believe this is really what the left wants, but this is
exactly what we'll get if we're not careful. Open the border;
then watch as the populations of the border states swell by the
millions and these jurisdictions, under intense pressure from
their constituents—of all colors—*do* turn into police states,
throwing immigrants out of schools and hospitals and ignoring
their constitutional rights. After the immigrants have been
thus dispatched, stay tuned as the gunsights turn to certain
categories among the native-born, people who will be de-

scribed, perhaps, by euphemisms such as "nonproductive." Prop 187 and the situation Leslie Marmon Silko described above will look like practice runs by comparison. And *The Wall Street Journal* will have more cheap labor than it ever dreamed of. That's the world that the left's anticitizenship will help create, a lesson the left would do well to learn quickly.

Chapter 6

FAITH IN SOMETHING BETTER

Affirmative Action

One night in early 1995, I was watching an episode of "Crossfire." The topic was affirmative action, specifically, the cleverly named California Civil Rights Initiative, a ballot referendum proposal cooked up by two conservative academics designed to eliminate all affirmative action programs in state hiring, contracting, and college admissions. Bob Beckel and Pat Buchanan were hosting; Willie Brown, then the speaker of California's House of Delegates and the state's leading defender of the affirmative action status quo, argued the liberal viewpoint, while Dana Rohrabacher, the Orange County congressman who in his younger days had played in a folk group called the Goldwaters, stood for the conservatives.

This quartet lumbered through the usual motions, and the usual eruptions ensued. Then, toward the end, Buchanan said something that made me glance up from whatever it was I was reading (one can't devote one's full attention to "Crossfire").

There was Mr. Kulturkampf himself mounting the argument that it was the right wing in America that was for equal opportunity, which the left had perverted through its fealty to quotas and goals and timetables. He even went so far as to quote approvingly Dr. King's famous line about people being judged not by the color of their skin but by the content of their character.

This kind of talk had become a fairly standard Republican appetizer by 1995; what made it stark, not to say rather disgusting, was that the words were issuing from the mouth of the man who, years before and back when it mattered, had accepted the FBI line on King and called him a "divisive and polarizing figure." Nevertheless, one needed only to watch that exchange to understand why affirmative action is on the ropes (and to see why CCRI, which will be on the November 1996 ballot, seems likely to pass with a comfortable majority). Brown made some good points that night but on the whole, he just didn't have the rhetoric that could match the conservatives and sway the opinions of those voters whose minds weren't already made up. Because who can argue against something so crisply American as equal opportunity?

I doubt Buchanan or Rohrabacher or California Governor Pete Wilson or the two academics who designed CCRI truly believe in equality of opportunity. If they did, they'd be out there pushing a ballot referendum advocating, say, the equalization of per pupil spending between rich and poor school districts, something they'll never do. Equality of opportunity has never existed in this country, doesn't exist now, and won't in the foreseeable future. But as a goal it's powerfully compelling to most people, and not without reason. And in the debate over affirmative action, the right has successfully managed the conversation so that it, against all history and probability, represents and speaks for equality of opportunity, while the left speaks for . . . special interests? Protection of a group? Blacks, women, and other minorities? Diversity? Fill in the blank however you choose; you can't plug anything in there that can compete in the minds of voters—mostly, but by no means wholly, white voters—with an idea like equality of opportunity.

In the late '90s, just as the welfare laws are about to be re-written and the immigration laws reworked, so too is affirma-tive action about to be changed. Such has been the success of the right's rhetoric. How quickly and how thoroughly the right can dismantle affirmative action will depend on a number of things: the success of the California initiative, certainly; the level of public support for change; and the level of support from the interests that finance national politics, which is not so high as one might imagine at first glance, for reasons we'll get into below. And as with welfare and immigration, the left faces a basic choice: we can either dig in our heels and argue for the status quo, even though every indication is that the status quo will not hold, or we can try to find ways to redefine affirmative action on terms acceptable and to a majority of Americans.

Many thinkers, including some on the left, have offered ways to proceed on this issue; indeed, a survey of left literature over the last few years turns up more engaged and variegated thinking on affirmative action than on welfare or immigration. But somehow, when the argument spills from the pages of left-wing and liberal journals out into the realm of public head-butting with the right, the tendency is toward defensiveness and tired rhetoric.

A sad example of this presented itself in the summer of 1995, when the Board of Regents of the University of Cali-fornia system met to vote on ending affirmative action admis-sions. Needing an issue to bolster his failing presidential cam-paign, Governor Pete Wilson was pushing the action, and, since most of the regents had been appointed by Wilson and previous Republican governors, the measure's chance of passage was pretty strong from the start. But the president of the university system was opposed to the change, as were several regents, other political leaders, and of course a vocal contingent of students. So out to Sacramento flew Jesse Jackson, who requested and was granted more than the 15 minutes usually allotted to guest speakers. Jackson launched into a 45-minute diatribe in which he invoked Orval Faubus and George Wallace and warned the board that if you do this, we'll shut down your campuses and clog your streets. But his speech demonstrated not the slightest knowledge of minority enrollment levels at various U.C. schools, and dealt less with the facts of the matter at hand than with the wrath that would be visited upon the regents' heads should they vote against his wishes. Jackson's speech, one witness told me, changed the dynamic of the debate and not, from a pro-affirmative action point of view, for the better. When he led a group in singing "We Shall Overcome" in front of the regents, they disbanded the meeting and went into another room. Later, Jackson led a march down one of Sacramento's broad thoroughfares, trying to disrupt the regular comings and goings, but literally could not get arrested. The measure passed. After the fall semester started, the liberal U.C.-Berkeley student newspaper, the *Daily Californian*, endorsed the regents' vote. Jackson led a march that day, too. Life at U.C.-Berkeley carries on as before.

Jackson's performance before the Board of Regents exemplified the same limitations that have characterized the left's arguments on welfare and immigration—25-year-old rhetoric, criticisms without alternative ideas. Some opponents of CCRI, hoping to avoid a replay of the Prop 187 debacle, did vow to place on the ballot an alternative measure. But as of this writing, none has materialized, meaning that California voters will probably be left with a choice between something extreme

(CCRI) and nothing. Unless new arguments are found and unless well-intended suggestions about new paths are heeded with sympathy and attention rather than dismissed out of hand, we'll be stuck in the mud once again.

Jackson before the Board of Regents, Willie Brown on "Crossfire," and affirmative action defenders in general try to cast affirmative action as being of a piece with—and thus as unassailable as—the civil rights laws of the mid-'60s. The truth is that affirmative action today is an ambiguous enterprise, both practically and morally. In practice, it has contributed to more racial mixing and is partially responsible for the more integrated society in which we now live, although no one can be sure how responsible. Nor has the question of whether it helps those who need help least, or leaves behind those who need help most (two slightly different things), been satisfactorily settled. But it's in moral terms that affirmative action's authority has most dissipated. Affirmative action was well-grounded and morally justified as a reparations policy for aggrieved black Americans; but somewhere over the years, it changed from a reparations policy to a diversity policy directed not only at black Americans, but at women, Latinos, and any and all minority groups, even some with little realistic claim to historic discrimination, at least not on the scale faced by black Americans. A diversity policy of this sort—maintained not by popular opinion but by court orders and executive mandates—became harder and harder to justify. And in an era when everyone faced declining wages and job security, it was probably inevitable that the current challenges to it would arise.

The salient points in affirmative action's history are well known. Executive orders under Kennedy and (especially) Johnson, Supreme Court decisions like *Griggs v. Duke Power Co.* (1971), and the various Nixon administration decrees that gave it life have been reviewed in many places. The goals have been twofold: first, to give black Americans and, later, women and other minorities opportunities in education and employment that historically they'd been denied (and hardly anyone these days, even on the extreme right, would try to argue that they were not denied those opportunities), and second to integrate society.

According to Harvard professor Randall Kennedy, "affirmative action has strikingly benefited blacks as a group and the nation as a whole" and has enabled blacks "to attain occupational and educational advancement in numbers and at a pace that would otherwise have been impossible." Numerical comparisons are not terribly easy to come by because, as Susan Clayton and Faye Crosby point out in *Justice, Gender, and Affirmative Action*, "it is difficult to separate out the effects of a particular policy from the effects of general social and economic change." Nevertheless, Clayton and Crosby have an apposite yardstick in a study comparing the number of women and minorities employed by businesses that have contracts with the federal government with the number employed by firms that don't (the former, of course, are required to establish hiring programs that benefit minorities and women). Between 1974 and 1980, firms that contracted with the federal government had work forces that were 20 and 15 percent minority and women, respectively, whereas the figures for noncontractors were 12 and 2 percent.

By this measure, and by other measures such as the increasing proportion of minorities and women in various professions, affirmative action is succeeding marvelously. One really need only watch television to confirm this, by taking note of the number of minority and female newscasters or the presence of minorities in advertising images (often the result not of accident or the good will of advertisers, but of a few lawsuits) or even the high profile in the O.J. Simpson trial of an African

American defense attorney, a black prosecutor, a female prosecutor, and an Asian American judge. Of course, the trial being
an explosive racial issue, each side had to get its racial house
in order: the County of Los Angeles could scarcely have afforded, in this day and age, to let three white men prosecute a
black football star. The racial balance of that courtroom would
never have existed 20 years ago, and it's no doubt the case
that affirmative action helped all of them, to one degree or another, pursue their professions. And though few places may be
as multicultural as Los Angeles, the diversity of that courtroom is duplicated in courtrooms and offices and hospitals
around the country.

The effect of this influx, it seems to me, is something of
which the left does not make quite enough hay. That is, the
left has tended to focus its arguments more on what affirmative action has done for its beneficiaries than on what it has
done for society as a whole. Yet affirmative action has undeniably helped integrate the country. And this integration, in
turn, has helped improve race relations in the population as
a whole. A few numbers, from a 1991 Gallup/*Newsweek* poll:
more than two-thirds of whites and 80 percent of blacks say
they "know many members of another race well"; 47 percent
of whites and 63 percent of blacks say they "socialize regularly
with members of another race"; 72 percent of blacks and
52 percent of whites would prefer to live in a mixed neighborhood; only 6 percent of whites say they'd be "uncomfortable"
working with or for someone of another race. These surveys
may tend to be overly rosy, but they still suggest that the races
do mix at reasonably high levels. When individual whites and
blacks, and men and women, begin to study and work together, stereotypes are countered and bigotry inevitably sub-
sides. Even those black and white co-workers who don't
socialize much have to interact with each other for the seven
or eight hours that constitute the work day and develop at

least collegial relationships. Given how segregated the country's neighborhoods still are, this kind of social mixing at work and at school can only be for the good. Points such as these have not been adequately made by the left; nor has it stressed that this particular remedy has brought about a less divided society. As Randall Kennedy, in the essay quoted above, notes, the integration forced by affirmative action has taught "whites that blacks, too, are capable of handling responsibility, dispensing knowledge, and applying valued skills."

Kennedy also points out that there isn't much evidence that integration would have proceeded as it has without affirmative action. Indeed, evidence exists to the contrary; without affirmative action, for example, the American legal profession would still be overwhelmingly white and male, instead of being nearly 30 percent female and 10 percent black as it now is (10 percent may sound low, but remember that blacks constitute 13 percent of the population). Further, without affirmative action, retrogression would be a fearful possibility, not because white employers would return to pre-civil rights era attitudes—the country has changed too much for that—but because people still tend to know and trust their own kind, and the unofficial network of contacts is not yet very integrated. In 1989, in *Croson v. Richmond*, the Supreme Court struck down minority set-asides in governmental contracting (that is, the setting aside of a certain percentage, usually around 30 percent, of all local public contracts for firms owned by minorities and women. Ever since, the percentage of contracts awarded to such firms has been plummeting—in Richmond itself, for example, from 35 percent to 1 percent. In other words, municipalities were not awarding contracts to minority firms because they believe in peace, love, and harmony. The law made them do it, and without the law, they're not doing it.

On the other hand, it should be noted that some racial progress may *not* be the result of affirmative action. In cities, many blacks and other minorities have joined the middle class through public sector employment. This may be less a matter of affirmative action than of simple ethnic succession; that is, just as the Irish, Jews, and Italians before them rose to middle-class status in some measure because of their infiltration of the public sector (Irish: police; Italians: fire and sanitation; Jews: social services), so now are blacks and Latinos filling those jobs. As whites left the cities, it was inevitable that minorities would start to take these positions—de facto affirmative action by attrition. Of course, it's possible that these minority-group members were in a position to take these jobs in part because of affirmative action college admissions. There seems never to have been a comprehensive study of this, but the point is that affirmative action probably can't claim all the credit for the existence of a larger black middle class.

Similarly, it's unclear how deeply affirmative action really has reached into society. A point conceded even by many on the left is that for all its successes, affirmative action is less a cure than a palliative, helping some people into the elite and leaving others far behind. Further, that elite, by the inclusion of a few people of color, is not changed in any essential way; that is, a corporate world ruled by dishonesty and cupidity, whose aims are fundamentally at odds with the needs of most working people, is still, even when its leading firms hire a few women and people of color, a corporate world ruled by dishonesty and cupidity, whose aims are fundamentally at odds etc. etc. Corollary to all this is the idea that affirmative action has in the end served a quite useful purpose to the country's elites, salving the consciences of law partners and CEOs and university administrators—not to say liberal politicians—across the country as the fundamental problems of poverty remain unattended to. Another criticism is that affirmative action lowers the self-esteem of recipients, who may feel that they have "made it" not on their merits but because they're black (or female or whatever, as the case may be). Finally, the criticism that affirmative action *does* have victims—white men who are denied jobs—leads into a debate about the moral efficacy of race-based as opposed to race-neutral remedies.

Let's have a look at these. Is affirmative action just a Band-Aid solution, lifting a few and leaving others behind? The answer is complicated. Clearly, the main effect, at least as far as African Americans are concerned, has been to help create a black middle class. Middle class is a purposively amorphous concept in this country, but various measures indicate that 40 to 60 percent of all black Americans are now middle class, up from around 12 or 15 percent 30 years ago. How much of this is the result of affirmative action is hard to say, but surely it deserves some of the credit. After all, increased minority enrollment in college has been central to affirmative action, and a college education generally leads to stability, leisure time, job options, career advancement, and disposable income—all the factors that make someone middle class. Yet black blue-collar workers have benefited as well; the *Griggs* decision held that employers could not set standards for employment that were even unintentionally discriminatory. In the wake of that decision, such blue-collar employers as Bethlehem Steel and AT&T were forced to refashion hiring in such a way that many more minorities and women were brought into the work force.

Still, black poverty has grown, and in some ways seems more incurable than ever. This leads some thinkers to the conclusion that affirmative action was perhaps just the best compromise available at the time to the problem of ensuring widescale social justice. As Cornel West has argued:

Progressives should view affirmative action as neither a major solution to poverty nor a sufficient means to equality. We should see it primarily playing a negative role—namely, to insure that discriminatory practices against women and people of color are abated.

West is obviously using "negative" in its rights-associated connotation and not to mean deleterious. He goes on to say that he supports affirmative action, in no small part for the reasons stated above: without it, West feels, discrimination "will return with a vengeance." Nevertheless, West's argument is essentially that affirmative action is worth defending only until a real consensus for something better is found.

If affirmative action is wanting as a means to equality, it surely is equally unsound as a means of changing the conduct of business in any significant way. Peter Gabel, writing in *Tikkun* magazine, argued that whereas at its best the civil rights movement challenged people to find their better selves and helped redefine society in a deeply moral sense, affirmative action, even at its best, does little more than incorporate previously excluded groups into the rat race. For Gabel,

> Affirmative action today implicitly affirms the idea that the goal of life is to make as much money and get as much status as possible in a market of scarce opportunities, and that people generally succeed in this competitive struggle according to their own merit, measured by more or less objective criteria. This is the background framework of social meaning against which people are expected to measure their success in life, their ultimate sense of self-worth.

Gabel writes that he, like West, would not oppose current affirmative action policies in lieu of something better. But his view is clear that affirmative action does more to recolor the world than to transform it (unlike a strict identity-based analysis, his does not presume that to recolor is by definition to transform). His analysis is perhaps a touch starry-eyed; people do have to make a living, after all, and it's not as though every black person or white woman who gains admittance to a good university is there to hustle a degree and go make a fast buck, any more than all white men seek to do that. Nevertheless, re-making the world in a more humane way, trying to bring people more liberty and leisure, must be at the center of any left program. If affirmative action does not meet that test, it's a limitation that must be acknowledged.

Which leads to the argument that affirmative action, far from presenting a challenge to ruling elites, is a development with which they are in fact quite comfortable. Why? Because elevating a relatively small number of minorities and women into the professions helps buy off more serious dissent. As the journalist Alexander Cockburn (another supporter of affirmative action in lieu of a better way) observed in 1995: "We end up with the left accepting tokenism and celebrating it as diversity." That may be too harsh, but the point, especially given poverty statistics, is well taken. Indeed, it is for these basic reasons that corporate America tends to have little quarrel with affirmative action. When Republican governors like William Weld of Massachusetts and Tom Ridge of Pennsylvania, among others, told congressional Republicans in the summer of 1995 that affirmative action simply wasn't a pressing issue in their states, they were in part signalling that their states' businesses—that is, their own financial benefactors—didn't need to be confused by new rules regarding a system with which they'd grown comfortable (remember, "diversity training" is by now a huge industry).

These critiques of affirmative action have been made by figures on the left (although observers elsewhere on the spectrum have made them as well). The two remaining criticisms— the self-regard of recipients and the question of affirmative action's white male victims—are more regularly advanced by those in the center and on the right. But they merit attention, particularly the second point, because the socially divisive aspects of

the policy, which even affirmative action's most ardent proponents cannot deny, get to heart of the need to search for better
alternatives.

I suspect that the self-esteem of those who benefit from affirmative action is more often helped than harmed; being
refused admission to college, after all, is more damaging
than being accepted with SATs that aren't quite up to snuff.
In this regard Nicholas Lemann, writing for *The New York
Times Magazine*, looked up a certain Dr. Patrick Chavis. It was
Chavis who gained admission to the U.C.-Davis medical
school instead of Allan Bakke, launching Bakke's lawsuit and
the noted Supreme Court decision. Chavis, who lives in the
tough Compton area of Los Angeles and whose practice provides primary care to poor people, isn't stigmatized in the
slightest. "If anything," Lemann writes, "he seems to assume a
superiority over his white medical-school classmates. He says
he works harder than they do and in tougher conditions." Undoubtedly true, to which one might add that no one raises the
stigma issue when the recipients of affirmative action are
white—which is the case at universities with loose regional
quotas and "legacy" admissions of alumni children (legacy is
the biggest affirmative action program on campuses today).

Still, it's wrong to dismiss this as a concern. Law professor
Stephen Carter and journalist Richard Rodriguez have made
the opposite point, and they are by no means "conservative"
just because they make it, as some critics have asserted. Both
have offered personal testimony that they at times felt as if
their white classmates looked down on them for being at elite
universities "only" because of their race. Carter refused acceptance to Harvard Law because he was turned down and
then hastily admitted a few days later after Harvard learned he
was black. The journalist Ruben Navarette, Jr., wrote mov-
ingly in his memoir, *A Darker Shade of Crimson*, of being told
by his high school principal that he might have a shot at Har-

vard—where he was indeed accepted—because of his minority status; never mind that he had straight A's throughout high school. Such situations are bound to arise, and an identity left that classifies people by their race and ethnicity rather than their more general humanity is partly to blame.

A more serious issue is the extent to which colleges and employers lower standards to facilitate minority representation. Colleges do lower their test-score standards to allow for the acceptance of more students of color, who tend to score lower than whites for reasons having to do with class and culture. This need not be a bad thing; indeed, test scores are dramatically overvalued, and the argument that standardized testing should be eliminated completely—and that college admissions should instead be based on a more well-rounded view of a student's background, interests, and potential—is tantalizing. But in some cases, standards have been outright perverted. The criticism that a degree from the City College of New York, once called "the Harvard of the poor," has been devalued makes New York progressives bristle, but there is much truth to the claim. Moreover, the entire City University of New York system, comprising more than 20 campuses, must accept any applicant. Given terribly low standards in the city's public schools, where students are passed because to hold them back is thought too stigmatizing, one can fairly ask whether those students are being ill served by an essentially patronizing system that refuses to hold them to rigorous standards and hands them diplomas even though they may read at eighth- or tenth-grade levels. Open admissions, as the policy is called, was rushed into place in 1970 in the wake of campus protests, and though more New York students may have received degrees as a result, the burden of accepting all applicants has left CUNY gasping for air. This is affirmative action going overboard, and it will soon give rise to its opposite: within a few years, open admissions will no doubt end, some

CUNY campuses will close or drastically cut back their operations (needless to say, money is tight now, too), and gradually,
vital middle-class public support for an extremely important
public institution will erode, though hopefully not to the van-
ishing point.

At least open admissions has the benefit of being race-
neutral (although, as a practical matter, it was instituted to
bring more students from the overwhelmingly black and Hispanic public schools into the system). This brings us to what is
really the central criticism of affirmative action: namely, that
race-specific remedies for past discrimination have run their
course and have antagonized a white working class whose
wages and job security have steadily eroded since the 1970s,
and that they must now be viewed as antithetical to the
American goal of a society that is truly egalitarian and hence
colorblind. The left tragically dismisses this as racism thinly
disguised and, in the hands of some conservatives, it probably
is. But it's a deeply serious question that many have asked in
good faith, and it deserves more thoughtful consideration than
the left has given it.

It may well be, as affirmative action's defenders claim, that
reverse discrimination is grossly exaggerated and that most reverse discrimination suits, once they reach the hard proving
ground of the courtroom, have no merit. But it is undeniably
the case that affirmative action, even as it has helped integrate
the country, has been divisive and lacks popular support.
Public opinion is opposed to preferential treatment for deprived groups. Nothing should be supported or opposed simply
on the basis of public opinion, but that opinion is surprising
and should make one take a step back. For example, in a
March 1995 *Washington Post* survey, 75 percent of those polled
said they oppose preferences on the basis of past discrimination. That included 81 percent of whites and 46 *percent* of
blacks. Other surveys have produced similar findings, suggest-

ing that black Americans, rather than reflexively supporting this policy, have given the issue deep thought—and that civil rights groups that toe the status quo line on affirmative action are rather badly out of touch with nearly half the constituency they claim to represent. Pluralities and even majorities of white women—who have benefited more from affirmative action than have blacks or any other group—also have expressed opportunity to race- and gender-based preferences.

The explanation for these results, as with the cross-racial support for Proposition 187 discussed in the previous chapter, cannot be that all these people are a bunch of yahoo racists and sexists. That simply does not compute with many other findings, such as those that show majorities of whites and blacks supporting racial mixing in its various forms. Part of the opposition to preferences is no doubt based on economic anxiety, particularly among working-class white men—which argues for class-based preference programs that do not take account of race, a topic to which I'll return.

But part of it surely must be that racial and gender preferences do not square with what most people—male, female, black, white, Hispanic, and so on—envision as the fulfillment of American society's best potential. And this is at the heart of affirmative action's moral ambiguity. Put bluntly: is affirmative action a moral imperative or a moral blot? The best moral claim that can be made for affirmative action is as a reparations policy, and it's a strong one. To put a slightly different spin on an old argument, consider the literal cash cost to black America of slavery and Jim Crow and official and unofficial segregation: the job chances and wages lost, the entrepreneurial openings denied, the education denied, the medical care denied, the housing denied, the property left to rot or burn by white owners, the bank loans never given, the jobs proffered always, until very recently, at the bottom of the wage structure. Each of these affected millions of people, from the founding of the republic (and we could go back further, of course) until, for all reasonable purposes and for all but a few, the 1970s, when affirmative action really kicked in. What are those losses worth, to put it in terms easily comprehensible to the lawyer, businessman, and insurance adjustor, in cash? Untold billions. In this respect, white society has only just begun paying black people back. Gertrude Ezorsky, in her *Racism and Justice: The Case for Affirmative Action*, argues:

> From a backward-looking perspective, blacks have a moral claim to compensation for past injury . . . If the effects of [slavery] had been dissipated over time, the claim to compensation now would certainly be weaker. From the post-Reconstruction period to the present, however, racist practices have continued to transmit and reinforce the consequences of slavery. Today blacks still predominate in those occupations that in a slave society would be reserved for slaves.

To affirmative action's strongest supporters, the argument pretty much begins and ends here. White society owes black society, as they say, big-time. And even those on the left who harbor reservations about the policy, like some of those quoted above, eventually land on this point as the basic justification for it.

White society *does* owe black society big-time, and reparations are morally necessary. But today, affirmative action is not a reparations policy; it's a diversity policy. It became a diversity policy during the 1970s, as it was expanded from a program for the uplift of black Americans into a program designed to serve more and more underrepresented groups brought within its ambit. So affirmative action now includes people in several other categories. What about them? White women face discrimination in this country, but is it anywhere near on a par with what blacks have faced? I've no doubt that Latinos are subjected to difficulties here, but America did not enslave them for 250 years (and they did come here by choice). Aleuts certainly face hardships, but does white America owe Aleuts what it owes blacks? It clearly does not. I wouldn't say that women, Latinos, Aleuts, and the rest deserve no preferential treatment whatever; it's just that their claim on white America's conscience is not remotely the same as blacks'. Affirmative action practiced similarly for all these groups has a far less certain moral claim to make than one that seeks to atone explicitly for the peculiarly horrid history of white treatment of blacks.

I do not suggest that affirmative action be limited to black Americans only. Such a program would probably have even less chance than the current one does of surviving politically, since including women, Latinos, and all the others expands the program's constituency and brings it that much more support. Besides, diversity is a good thing. But where do its demands logically stop, and why? The expansion of affirmative action into a diversity policy has, without question, helped many women, Latinos, and others, and thereby helped society as a whole; but it may also have hardened the opposition to affirmative action, and it has certainly made affirmative action more difficult to defend. Recall the remark by Henry Louis Gates, Jr., that a Polish policeman's grandmother could offer "poignant firsthand testimony" to the discrimination Poles faced in America. If affirmative action covers, say, the daughter of a wealthy Cuban American building contractor, why should it not cover the son of a poor white coal miner from eastern Kentucky? The distinctions become more and more nebulous, more and more hair-splitting, and more and more obsessed with ranking disadvantage solely on the basis of ethnicity and gender. It's true that a white male usually has certain built-in advantages, but only usually. What about the unusual cases, which, as jobs go south and wealth becomes ever more concentrated, are becoming not so unusual?

The left hasn't dealt squarely with such questions. The simple demand that affirmative action be continually expanded to include newly discovered out-groups, proceeding from the simple assumption that all white males, regardless of their station, constitute one huge in-group, just can't hold. It's not practically the case, and it's not morally right. The attempt to pull the price of past discrimination out of the hides of people who were not responsible for it is an ambiguous undertaking. And issues have a way of connecting themselves to each other. For example, a policy of affirmative action for diversity's sake cannot long coexist with a policy of open immigration, as the political scientist Jim Chapin has observed. Why should a woman from Argentina or a man from Antigua, both fresh on these shores, be beneficiaries of affirmative action? Public opinion—and not just white public opinion—will never support that, and it should not be expected to.

A second central problem the left has not acknowledged forthrightly is that affirmative action has integrated society more as a matter of bureaucratic and legal coercion than as a call to a set of higher principles and beliefs. No national case was ever made for affirmative action; it was never a bottom-up movement, but always a top-down one, and all this was by design. As Lemann noted in his *New York Times Magazine* article, affirmative action arose not out of a mass movement that produced legislation but from presidential executive orders and court decisions. Legislation—the great civil rights bills of the '60s, say—subjects issues to broad public debate. Such debate, for all its superficiality and vulnerability to being hijacked by filibustering senators and the like, forced civil rights proponents to make their case to the public, and their case won the day. Executive orders and court decisions are not reflected in debate's glare and so, as Lemann says, "the muscles that liberals would have used to make a public case for affirmative action atrophied—and the conservatives' were becoming magnificently buffed and toned." Liberal and leftist proponents of affirmative action sought to avoid the debate, Lemann says, because they believed that "you could never trust Congress to do the right thing on racial matters" (even though it did through much of the '60s).

So affirmative action, while part of the '60s civil rights legacy, was in crucial respects a shadow piece of the agenda. The fact, well established in the memoirs of aides such as John Ehrlichman, that Nixon supported it mainly because he knew it would drive a deep wedge between two key Democratic constituencies—civil rights groups and labor—suggests that affirmative action was sustained and enforced for four crucial years (that is, during Nixon's first term, after which he dropped his support) precisely to wreak havoc and spark dissension.

Reliance on the courts and bureaucracies to make social change for which there is little popular support, and for which a national case has not been compellingly made, will sometimes succeed in forcing that change for shorter periods or longer; but it will *always* succeed in strengthening the opposition to such change. And, having lost the public argument, the left has turned to litigating social change as its staple—not only on affirmative action, but on issues as various as special education and prisoners' comforts and the right to beg in public places and a vast array of environmental concerns, with the result that court-mandated relief is forcing government at all levels to spend billions of dollars on programs that voters hardly know exist, let alone ever considered and approved.

Frank Deale, a radical lawyer who has devoted much of his life to such litigation, spoke of the limitations of such strategies in an interview he gave to the *Socialist Review* in 1991:

> If the law can bring about collective goals—and I don't necessarily believe that it can—it would have to be a reflection of a massive political movement. I've learned a lot from the experi-

ence of working on litigation of the type designed, for example, to end U.S. aid to El Salvador. We lost that particular case, because the Court said the relief you're trying to get can only be provided by Congress, and if you really feel that the extent of human rights violations in El Salvador is such that the United States shouldn't be providing aid to that country, you've got to persuade 535 or so people in Congress of that argument.

That's of course much harder to do, but in the long run there's something to be said for it. People ask me, why look to the courts as a shortcut for educational work? And other than just falling back on my role as a lawyer representing clients, I don't always have an answer for them. If in fact we're living in a society where there is space for people to organize and speak and agitate and petition their government, why shouldn't those big political struggles for collective rights come out of that process, rather than the litigation process? That's always been one of the toughest questions I've faced.

Deale, who in the same interview gave affirmative action mixed notices, recognizes what defenders of the affirmative action status quo refuse to: the courts can dictate a solution, even provide a "victory" here and there, but they cannot sustain social change if the mass of people don't support it. Persuading the "535 or so" people in Congress—which really means persuading their constituencies, which is to say, public opinion—requires arguments that appeal to people's consciences and that evoke a vision of democratic promise fulfilled, especially on an issue so near the raw nerve of race. Affirmative action, always limited in its aims and saddled with its own contradictions, has proved incapable of doing that.

But what about the specter, which Cornel West raises, of racism returning "with a vengeance" if affirmative action is undone? What about the post-*Croson* statistics from Richmond, of minority contracts dropping from 35 to 1 percent? They're disastrously regressive, and shouldn't be tolerated. But it could be that the set-aside goals were unrealistically high in the first place. Most municipalities stipulated that 30 percent of contracts be set aside for minority- and women-owned firms. Yet in very few municipalities do minorities and women own 30 percent of the businesses that bid for contracts (indeed, shell minority-owned firms—companies that put a Latino or black at the top of the letterhead to help their contract business—exist everywhere). This, too, is a problem, but it's a different one; this is the problem of the lack of access to capital that so many black people and other minorities face. The University of California regents, in rescinding racial preferences, passed a resolution that continues to emphasize "commitment to diversity" as a U.C. goal. Will black and Latino enrollment remain at current levels? No; everyone concedes they'll go down, although by how much is debated. But black and Latino enrollment levels in the U.C. system aren't that high now— about 5 and 15 percent, respectively. It's obvious that the real problem is not that admission policies aren't liberal enough racially, but that black and Latino children are provided an inferior and badly funded public education.

Correcting the lack of access to capital and the imbalances in public education requires a program more radical than affirmative action, as does correcting the vast inequities and difficulties that millions of working people face. But we can be sure that affirmative action supporters like the Clintons and most other Democrats would never undertake such a program, because doing so would require taking on the real culprits. And the Clintons, like the Democratic Party as a whole, are too dependent on the largesse of those culprits' political action committees. The journalist Jim Sleeper asked rhetorically, "Do white liberals . . . champion race-specific remedies as sops to conscience, precisely because they have no intention of challenging the deeper inequities and exploitations that divide not only whites from blacks but also whites from one another?" The answer is an obvious and resounding yes.

Of course, the left can't cashier affirmative action on the right's terms, of which a prime example is the California initiative. Proposals like that must be fought. The argument that government should be "out of the race business entirely" is phony. As long as there are jobs to fill and contracts to award—that is to say, forever—the government will be in the race business, because someone will be getting those jobs and contracts and someone else won't. But what the left must do in the long run, as I've argued since this book's opening pages, is produce an answer that (1) lays out a real and unifying program and (2) speaks in plain language to the mass of voters and convinces them of the value of our arguments. I hardly need to point out, given public opinion on the issue today, that the failure to do so will almost surely result in affirmative action's being cashiered on precisely the right's terms.

There are ways to do this. The most hopeful suggestions for alternatives to affirmative action have come from some on the left but mainly from thinkers like William Julius Wilson who are more often called liberal or moderate. No doubt this prevents many who regard themselves as the last true representatives of the real left from considering their proposals. But Wilson's well-known call, which he's been making since the late 1970s, for universal remedy programs that address black poverty but also help working-class and poor whites has to be heeded. He points out, rightly, that "only with multiracial support could programs of social and economic reform get approved in Congress." Sociologist Theda Skocpol is another who has argued the merit of race-neutral programs and their potential ability to "promote equality and to revitalize democratic cross-racial political coalitions in the 1990s." And Richard Kahlenberg made a solid case for such an approach in *The New Republic*. I would suggest not that class become the sole criterion for affirmative action programs, but that it be included as part of a formula that continues to rely on race, gender, and ethnicity to some extent. So, for example, if a poor black person and a poor white person are competing for a spot and their qualifications are roughly equal, extra consideration should be given to the black person. What happens when it's a middle-class person of color competing against a poor white? The permutations of such competitions are endless, and the answer to the question of how to address them is that it depends; the real world requires complex judgments, and hard and fast rules don't work. Clearly, there are still some situations in which discrimination is all but blatant—in some police and fire departments, for example, and some unions; in these cases, a firm line must be drawn. The point is that care must be taken so that black concerns are not relegated to some kind of secondary status, but black and white concerns should be made one and the same, with a class-tinged fillip that hopefully would be appealing to leftists.

Former New York City schools chancellor Ramon Cortines introduced a plan that serves as an example of a way to proceed. It may shock outsiders to learn that, despite general trends, New York City is still home to a few of the finest public high schools in the country—Stuyvesant in lower Manhattan and the Bronx High School of Science are the best known. Students who attend these schools are virtually assured that life's various doors will swing wide open to them. Of course, admission is highly competitive and enrollment has been almost exclusively white and Asian. Before Mayor Giuliani bullied him out of town, Cortines established an academy for promising, low-income preteens designed to prepare them for the rigors of these high schools. The goal, of course, is to raise

minority enrollment (which the school will do if it's well-run).
But it is not an explicitly race-based program—15 percent of
the children in the first class were white—and does not seek
to raise minority enrollment through the courts or the impo-
sition of quotas. Children who perform well at the preparatory
academy will almost certainly perform well at the elite high
schools; they will, in other words, not have to deal as much
with self-esteem questions because they'll be able to do the
work. Compare this with the legal, practical, and ethical mess
of San Francisco's high school admissions programs, which are
based firmly on quotas and have created deep interracial tension. Of course, when a few white students are actually displaced from Bronx Science in favor of graduates of Cortines'
academy there will be some complaints, but those can be more
easily isolated because no one will be able to say that on merit,
the minority kids don't deserve to be there.

This is the sort of program the left needs to propose. It is
specific, it values diligence as well as disadvantage, its goal is
one with which few people would disagree, and it acheives the
goal by means of a plan that is rooted in fairness and opportunity. Per pupil funding in public education and the fundamental question of how public education is financed—mostly
through property taxes, which is why wealthy suburbs can
spend $10,000 per child while some poorer areas, both urban
and rural, spend perhaps $3,000—is another issue the left
should press. Again, a program to address this blatantly unfair
system would not be race-based per se—the white child in the
Ozarks would benefit as much as the black child in Roxbury—
but would certainly help lift minority children and give them a
better chance. Programs like these, guided by principles like
these, have the potential to pull together a mighty coalition.

Such programs, and an attempt to put together such a coalition, require from the left some degree of faith in the mass of
people to be fair and make reasonable moral judgments. They

require, also, faith in democracy's resilience, its elasticity, and its absorptive powers. Having faced far more venom and violence than any civil rights leaders face today, King and his contemporaries never lost that faith. They were not naive about the depth of racism or the intractability of the ruling elites, and they never brushed aside or downplayed racism; but they believed that most people, confronted with hard evidence and compelling moral arguments, could overcome racism and think and act in a better way. The left has no such faith right now, which is why people have no faith in us.

Chapter 7

ARMIES UNCONSIDERED

Health Care

S ometime in late 1992, after Bill Clinton was elected but
before he took the oath of office, there was a rally in Little
Rock, Arkansas, where the president-elect was busily sorting
through resumes and position papers. Although the rally drew
about a thousand people, it was little noted in the major
media; I learned of it in *Nation's Health*, a weekly newspaper
devoted to health care issues. The rally was struck to promote
a single-payer health care plan, the system by which the federal government would direct health care—would become, in
the argot, the "single payer" of reimbursements to health care
providers.

Under single-payer, health care would no longer be tied to
employment and would thus be universal; the payment of insurance premiums, which now finance health care for all
Americans except those on Medicare and Medicaid, would
end and be replaced by taxes. There being no insurance pools

or health maintenance organizations under single-payer, people would be free to choose whatever primary care doctors they liked. Everyone would receive the same basic care, at little out-of-pocket cost, although those who had the money to do so could buy supplemental coverage. Finally, since there would be no premiums, there would be no need for health insurance as we know it, so insurance companies would be out of the health care business. Canada uses a single-payer system (as do some Western European countries), and though health care there is obviously not perfect, far more Canadians—both recipients *and* doctors—profess satisfaction with their system than do their American counterparts; and it costs far less. Insurance companies, of course, are probably less satisfied.

We don't know whether the Clintons paid any attention to that rally, but we do know from subsequent events that they did everything they could to run away from the single-payer proposal. In fact, Bill Clinton already had run away from it as a candidate, supporting on the stump either managed care or so-called play or pay schemes. And run away as well did the insurance and medical lobbies, *The New York Times* and other influential newspapers, and most elected officials. On the right, Republican proposals consisted of variants of the above two schemes or were centered around the concept of medical "savings accounts," which would set the amount a family or individual could spend on health care each year and refund any unused balance.

The failure of the Clinton health plan, for which any hope of passage shut down in August 1994, set off one of those orgies of postmortem punditry that Washington reserves for just a handful of topics each year: it was too complicated; it was a haphazard mishmash of aspects of several competing plans; it was (according to the right) "socialized medicine" (which was hogwash); it truckled (according to the left) to the interests of the large insurance companies (which was the truth). Clinton should have attacked welfare reform first, many argued; without such a preemptive nod to the right, there was no realistic hope of winning his nod to the left, which is what his plan was seen as being (whether it really was is well open to question). Whatever the Clinton plan was, one thing it was not was a plan that directly and simply addressed most Americans' concerns about health care. And so, when Congress adjourned for its summer recess that year and the Clintons whisked themselves off to Martha's Vineyard, they and the rest of us—an "us" that includes about 40 million uninsured people—were left to ponder the what ifs.

Looking back, *not* passing a healthcare bill—or even bringing one to a congressional vote—required monumental bungling. Health care is admittedly an immense and slothful beast to tame with one piece of legislation, but remember how the stage was set in 1991. In Pennsylvania, Democrat Harris Wofford won a special election for the U.S. Senate against Republican Richard Thornburgh—a former governor, the sitting attorney general, and the overwhelming favorite. Wofford won, after trailing by 40 points in early polls, by identifying and stressing one issue: health care. He was intentionally foggy on the details, but explicit in calling for a universal healthcare system that would insure everyone. Thornburgh kept silent on the issue until late October, when he pilloried universal coverage as "untried, untested, radical, and costly." He promptly shot down in the polls, which had been showing a statistical dead heat, and finished with 45 percent of the vote.

After Wofford's victory, health care legislation seemed as inevitable as the rising of the sun. A few plans were advanced in 1991, but a clueless George Bush—the man who bought socks in Frederick, Maryland, to prove he knew how regular people lived—didn't have any idea what to do. This swung the door wide open for Democrats, especially with an election—

the season of grand promises—approaching fast. Health care, further, was one of those few issues on which the public seemed to trust Democrats more than Republicans. Finally, with Clinton's election, Democrats controlled the White House and both houses of Congress. How could health care reform, still at or near the top of the voters' agenda, not reach fruition? True to form, the Clintons found a way.

Was the left culpable in this retreat? Not really. On welfare, on immigration, and on affirmative action, the left has been guilty of not having a strong program to present to the public, of critiquing conservative and liberal alternatives without offering any of its own. With respect to health care, it cannot be said, happily, that such was the case. The left had and has a position, and a good one: single-payer, while not without its own problems, would serve the interests of both middle-class and poor Americans in a variety of ways. Since coverage would not be contingent on employment, everyone would have coverage from birth and could choose their own doctors. Furthermore, several studies, from the respected Congressional Budget Office and elsewhere, have shown time and again how single-payer would save money by reducing overhead costs (if it sounds incongruous that government takeover of a private activity could save money, you must not know anything about the insurance business). The single-payer bill, spearheaded in the House by Washington's Jim McDermott and in the Senate by Minnesota's Paul Wellstone, ultimately accrued 93 House cosponsors—not a majority of Democrats, but a larger number than any of the other Democratic bills (save the president's) had. Most of all, single-payer had potential as an issue that working- and middle-class people of all colors and ethnicities could unite around, not against the poor or the immigrant but against a real culprit, the large insurance companies—which unlike the public are relatively happy with U.S. health care just the way it is.

If the left did make a mistake in the way it pushed single-payer, it was to place too much emphasis on the "37 million uninsured Americans"—the phrase was repeated so often it began to lose its impact—and too little emphasis on the vast army of working- and middle-class underinsured people, who live in fear that their coverage will be canceled or reduced or that it won't pay for their child's dental work. The 37 million are of course important—by and large, they're some of the poorest people in America, most of them working. But a strategy that emphasized both uninsured and underinsured alike would have spoken to a larger audience and might have paired poor and middle-class interests instead of isolating the poor as the only people whose interests the left had at heart.

But single-payer never really got around first base. The Clintons pooh-poohed it, other moderate Democrats followed suit, and the press sloughed it off as too radical for America. How and why did these things happen? And after single-payer was out of the picture, why was there no health care reform at all? For all the left's reservations about Clinton, healthcare reform was one area for which many held out some hope. Perhaps there's a lesson in that.

Progressive aspirations for a national health plan date back to at least 1912, when Theodore Roosevelt, running under the Bull Moose banner, incorporated it into his presidential platform. TR's nephew also supported a national health plan; it was to be a part of the New Deal as originally conceived, but the American Medical Association, even then, made known to FDR its rather strong feelings on the subject and Roosevelt backed off for fear that it might derail his larger program. In 1948, Truman proposed a national health bill, but similar forces kicked into gear to prevent its passage. And, as we saw in Chapter Two, it was part of Henry Wallace's platform. Kennedy concentrated not on national health care but on coverage for the elderly ("Try to stay young!" went the lampooning slogan of Kennedy impersonator Vaughn Meador). Kennedy, too, gave in before the power of the A.M.A., which raised the usual warnings about "Bolshevism" and "socialized medicine." It took the momentum of the Johnson administration and the 89th Congress to pass Medicare, providing government-financed coverage for the elderly, and Medicaid, the similar program that serves the very poor. Needless to say, the predicted Bolshevism did not arise; just the opposite, in fact, since the programs (in many instances) effectively converted the elderly and the poor from charity cases to paying customers, with the government shelling out the fees. A *New Yorker* cartoon from 1969 shows a physician paying for a yacht, in cash, and exclaiming, "And to think I opposed the passage of Medicare."

During the Nixon era, Teddy Kennedy was a leader in the push for national health; he, or someone on his staff, even wrote a book on the topic. In the mid-1970s, Oregon Congressman Al Ullman, who chaired the House Ways and Means Committee after Wilbur Mills's downfall, was so bold as to predict that Congress would pass, and President Gerald Ford would sign, national health legislation that would stipulate universal coverage for all Americans through a mix of employer mandates—that is, making employers provide health insurance to their workers—and an expanded federal role for the unemployed and others. It didn't happen, of course, for the same old reason: the power of the lobbies, particularly the A.M.A. and the various insurance lobbies. The Reagan and Bush years were predictably bleak. The only serious attention paid to health care delivery during those years was aimed at cutting costs; needless to say, most of the laws passed not only failed to reduce costs but also hindered service. During all this time, of course, public opinion polls showed immense popular support for national health care in one form or another; it's just that the public is no match for the opposition.

As reform efforts failed one after the other and as health care costs shot through the roof, some Americans—progressives to be sure, but others as well—looked to a country from which America, let's face it, typically does not receive much inspiration. But the Canadian single-payer system, consolidated into one national plan in 1971, had appeal for several reasons. In addition to the attributes noted above, the single-payer system in Canada kept health care costs under somewhat better control: Canada typically spends about 11 percent of its GNP on health care, while the United States spends almost 15 percent. In his 1984 presidential run, Jesse Jackson committed his campaign to a Canadian-style system. In 1988, with the leverage that came from collecting 6.5 million votes in the Democratic primaries, Jackson was able to force the Dukakis platform committee at the Democratic national convention to add a plank supporting national health care, though not necessarily a government-driven plan. True, a platform is just a platform, but at least it bespeaks some degree of recognition and attention.

Jackson deserves much credit for putting the single-payer alternative forward, but it took others to make the establishment pay more attention. In 1990, Chrysler chairman Lee Iacocca publicly noted that health care costs accounted for $700 of the price of every car made in America, while the figure for Canada was just $223 in U.S. currency (figures for other industrialized countries cited by Iacocca were similarly low). He expressed admiration for the Canadian system and suggested that perhaps we ought to take a look at it. Tellingly, his remarks were given far more prominence in Canadian than in American publications. Joseph Califano, Jr., was another establishment personage—a former Secretary of Health and Human Services—who looked to Canada and liked much of what he saw.

It might have been expected that Iacocca, so respected by many Americans, and Califano, so respected by Beltway types, would wield some influence on the public discussion. Certainly the A.M.A. feared as much; in 1989, sniffing the dangerously shifting winds, the group earmarked $2.5 million for a so-called Public Alert Program designed to tell Americans "the facts" about Canada's system. As researchers Theodore Marmor and Jerry L. Mashaw write, "the doctors' association placed advertisements in major media and supplied press kits for a blitz of editorials, opinion pieces, and reports about Canada. Similar essays began appearing in national and local papers by people identified as, for example, 'a surgeon from White Plains.'" A miniscandal over financing forced the cancellation of the campaign, but not before millions of Americans had "heard that Canadian health care doesn't work well and that, even if it did, it couldn't work in the United States."

The A.M.A. campaign was not, of course, the end of it. In 1990, a year before Wofford's victory, the campaign for U.S. Senate in Maine showed again how any talk of a Canadian model could scare the powers that be—and how susceptible such talk was, and is, to countervailing scare tactics. A Democrat named Neil Rolde, running against Republican incumbent William Cohen, made Canadian-style health care a centerpiece of his campaign—the first election to turn on health care as a major issue. Cohen and campaign consultant Bill McInturff knew just what to do. Their ad program featured scenes of long lines at a Department of Motor Vehicles office—the image of bureaucratic lethargy that probably makes more people shiver more than any other, with the possible exception of the post office. Said the voice-over: "This is your health care system if we go to a national plan." McInturff later bragged that his candidate's campaign had "trashed the hell out of the Canadian system," and Cohen, though slightly outspent by the wealthy Rolde, carried the day in a landslide.

Wofford's victory interrupted this trend and gave single-payer advocates a new opening. It must be noted that Wofford himself did not endorse a single-payer plan, talking instead in generalities. Still, the fact that Thornburgh was unable to do to Wofford what Bill Cohen had done to his opponent seemed to suggest that something had changed. The support for single-payer was in some respects broad, but it was always on the margins of so-called respectable opinion. The single-payer drive was spearheaded by several major unions, by Ralph Nader's Public Citizen group, and by more than 150 grassroots organizations. Certain other groups, such as Physicians for a National Health Program and the National Council of Senior Citizens, also supported single-payer, but their numbers were relatively small—the physicians' group has about 5,500 members, while the A.M.A.'s membership approaches 300,000. Among politicians, the much-maligned Jerry Brown was the only presidential candidate in 1992 to support single-payer, while other Democrats, including Clinton and most notably Paul Tsongas, dismissed it. On Capitol Hill, the leaders were McDermott, a former psychiatrist who was never among the most influential members of Congress, and Minnesota Senator Paul Wellstone, who does not have a terribly high reputation in Washington circles. These were, unfortunately, easy marks for the mainstream press either to ignore or deride, and so when a campaigning George Bush made the ridiculous assertion that Canada's health care system combined "the efficiency of the post office with the sensitivity of the KGB" and labeled it "a cure worse than the disease," he got away with it.

Canadians themselves, of course, were puzzled. *The New York Times*, which in its editorials had consistently knocked single-payer and backed managed competition, did work up the fortitude to run one piece in which Canadian providers and officials were permitted to speak up in defense of their system. Practically all of Bush's notions—exaggerated accounts of rationed service, waiting lists, and high administrative costs—were exposed for the nonsense that they were.

Dennis Timbrell, president of the Ontario Hospital Association, struck at the heart of the matter by pointing out that
Canadian health care cost less—at the time, $1,961 per
person, compared to $2,566 in the United States—because of
the "overwhelming duplication of bureaucracies working in
dozens of insurance companies in the United States, no two of
which have the same forms or even the same coverage." Of
course, American political discourse assumes that bloat and
inefficiency are solely features of the public sector. Anyone
who's ever had to call the offices of his or her insurance plan
to straighten something out knows better, but such are the
pinched parameters of public conversation.

The above paragraphs describe the milieu in which the
Clinton adminstration set about its work. Support existed for
a single-payer plan, but it paled in the face of its powerful opponents—the major lobbies, *The New York Times*, most mainstream politicians, the president-elect himself. Among the
public there existed broad support for universal coverage, but
whether that translated into support for a single-payer plan is
admittedly open to question. Numerous polls were taken, but
they don't mean that much: the lack of unanimity in their
findings was far greater than is usually the case, with the results depending on how questions were phrased, whether respondents were asked about just one plan or several, etc.
Several polls did show that the *features* of a single-payer
system—universal coverage, freedom to choose physicians,
contained costs—had broad support. But the label "single-
payer" had already taken such a whacking in the major media
that people often had a bad impression of it, perhaps without knowing that it advanced the very principles they said
they favored.

It was thus pretty easy for the Clintons to ignore single-
payer advocates, and by and large they did so. When Quentin
Young, a past president of Physicians for a National Health

Program and a past health adviser to Jesse Jackson, was sum-
moned to the White House in February 1993, it didn't take
long for him to realize that he'd been invited for, in his words,
a "pseudo-consultation." White House aide Walter Zelman
made it clear that the administration considered single-payer
to be "not politically feasible."

Around the same time, David Himmelstein of the Harvard
Medical School, and a longtime advocate of single-payer, met
with Hillary Rodham Clinton. After she heard him out, Mrs.
Clinton asked Himmelstein how he thought the White House
could beat the insurance industry. "With presidential leadership and polls showing that 70 percent of Americans favor the
features of a single-payer system," he replied. Her response:
"Tell me something new, David."

Were Hillary and Zelman right? Any honest analysis has
to conclude that they probably were, or at least that their
position was entirely rational from their perspective. What two
Roosevelts and a Truman couldn't do, two Clintons weren't
likely to accomplish. The White House was pinning a lot on
successful health care reform; even with all of Clinton's
equivocations and evasions and double-talk, successful passage of a health care program, *any* health care program, would
have ensured him lots of reelection support from the middle
and the left. The political decision to craft a careful and
not-too-radical plan was, admittedly, an understandable one.
Once the word came down from the Clintons, other leading
Democrats followed suit. Senate Majority Leader George
Mitchell, speaking informally with influential journalists in
July, said bluntly that single-payer "will not be enacted," and
so it went.

But as it turned out, the A.M.A. and insurance lobbies
fought the Clinton proposal with the same intensity they'd
have brought to a fight against single-payer. A political calcu-

lation to trim the sails is useful and defensible if, without sacrificing too much in the way of principle, it gets you more votes. The Clinton calculation did not do that. And in this instance, given the number of co-sponsors single-payer already had in the House of Representatives and the appeal of the plan's salient features, it may actually have been the case that a single-payer system could have been sold to the public. The seller, though, had to be willing to confront one of Washington's most powerful lobbies—something the Clintons weren't up to; but this, too, is something people clearly say they want their leaders to do more of.

When Clinton finally announced his own plan in September of 1993, his report outlined six principles: security, simplicity, savings, quality, choice, and responsibility. Those are precisely the principles single-payer supports, and though it is vulnerable to some attack on the question of quality, the charges leveled against it on this front, like all criticisms of single-payer, were grossly distorted. (The argument, in brief, is that advanced technology and specialty care in Canada lag behind the United States, and there does seem to be some truth to the claim.)

In the face of all this, single-payer advocates pressed forward, hoping to get the administration's plan to incorporate as many aspects of their bill as possible—in particular, they wanted a guarantee that coverage would be universal and that states would have the opportunity to adopt their own single-payer plans if they so chose. A *Times* article in May 1993, although it patronizingly described single-payer advocates as "guerilla fighters" seen by some as "hopeless idealists," nevertheless did allow that the single-payer coalition in the House was one the president couldn't afford to anger too much if he wanted his own plan to pass. The *New England Journal of Medicine*, interestingly enough, gave single-payer a boost through the spring and summer of 1993. Its editorial in April was favorable, and in August—when it was known that Clinton would be announcing his plan the next month—it published the results of a study, done by Himmelstein and his Harvard colleague Dr. Steffie Woolhandler, showing that paperwork accounted for fully 25 percent of American health care costs, more than double the percentage in Canada. The study held that the United States could save $50 billion in hospital costs, over and above other and larger administrative costs, by adopting a Canadian-style system, and it supplied the following eye-opening statistic: in 1968, U.S. hospitals cared for 1.378 million patients and employed 435,100 managers and clerks; by 1990, the number of patients was down to 853,000, while the number of employees had risen to 1.221 million.

That study, too, fell into the abyss. Finally, two weeks later, speaking before the National Governors' Association, Clinton laid out the rudiments of his plan; a month later, he unveiled his managed care proposal to Congress and the public. In one of the rare jousts by a single-payer supporter allowed on the *Times*'s op-ed page—the overwhelming majority of pro-single payer agitprop in the *Times* had been relegated to the letters columns—Melvin Konner, a doctor who teaches at Emory University, skewered the plan and showed again the advantages of a single-payer system. Clinton's proposal, contrary to the rhetoric, would limit physician choice because "managed care isn't profitable without administrative efficiency: the plan musn't deal with too many doctors. And that in turn means little or no choice." After noting that, in a 1993 newsletter, the Prudential Insurance Company had called managed competition its "best case scenario for reform," Konner wrote:

> The Clintons are creating an insurance business oligopoly that will own a seventh of the economy. Insurers are moving aggres-

sively into the delivery of care. Prudential, Metropolitan Life, Cigna and Aetna have each acquired H.M.O.'s and other managed-care companies that enroll millions of people.

This trend is likely to result in a vertical monopoly on America's health care, in which a few powerful insurers would control the delivery of care from the top down.

Konner wrote what everyone to Clinton's left knew to be the case; still, the left's opposition began to splinter as soon as Clinton announced his proposal into the expected we-should-work-with-him and we-should-keep-pushing camps. The only alternatives at this point were to try to bring the McDermott bill to the floor for a vote, even though it would never pass with a Democratic president against it, or to support Clinton publicly while privately trying to amend his proposal to make it as progressive as possible. Labor unions, by and large, fell into the accommodationist camp. This was at precisely the same point in time when Clinton was pushing NAFTA, bringing former presidents of both parties to Washington to help him argue the case. Labor opposed NAFTA vehemently, of course, and apparently decided to give the president's health plan qualified support so as not to appear too obstructionist. What labor appeared instead was weak.

The unions were following a perhaps understandable impulse to try to stay in the game: only by publicly saying kind things about the Clinton proposal could they hope to influence it. Other single-payer advocates agreed. Writing in *The Nation* in 1994, Naftali Bendavid looked back over the debacle and saw how the single-payer coalition had fallen apart in crucial ways, after Clinton announced his plan, into the two camps described above (there were also a few reformers who endorsed the Clinton proposal without reservation). Ralph Nader's Public Citizen, the grassroots group Neighbor to Neighbor, and a few unions like the Oil, Chemical, and

Atomic Workers took the harder line, while Citizen Action and the Consumers' Union sought compromise. The White House, of course, employed all the expected tricks, such as the invitations to Pennsylvania Avenue to "discuss policy." Old tricks, but they still work.

A few developments at least served to keep single-payer in the conversation. In December 1993, the Congressional Budget Office released another report demonstrating the cost savings that a single-payer program would provide. The CBO said this time that single-payer could save taxpayers $114 billion a year. In January 1994, McDermott and Wellstone announced their financing package, which included an 8.4 percent payroll tax on employers with more than 75 workers, a 4 percent tax on employers with fewer than 75 workers, and a 2.1 percent tax on workers' taxable income. Of course, this immediately opened the plan up to attack from conservatives and even from many Democrats who'd caught the antitax contagion. In reality, the tax was arguably less than what many people and employers already paid for their insurance premiums—Wellstone said most large business would actually see a savings from the roughly 12 percent of payroll that they would no longer have to pay in premiums. In February, representatives of the 60,000-member American College of Surgeons, testifying before Congress, announced "qualified approval" of single-payer. The same month, Jack Smith of General Motors told *The Washington Post* that he backed a single-payer system. In March, *Business Week* suggested that it might be time to give single-payer another look.

What was going on with the Clinton plan, in the meantime? The well-known and effective Harry-and-Louise ads, featuring the yuppie-ish couple who expressed various fears about the Clinton proposal, had already been on the air for several weeks. Bill and Hillary countered with some parody ads of their own, although these didn't really run as an ad campaign—they were seen only by journalists and other D.C. insiders at a dinner. The unions hauled out Stiller and Meara to do an ad. Stiller and Meara? Nothing against them, but couldn't the unions have enlisted someone a little more up-to-date? They probably had Shari Lewis and Lambchop ready for the next round.

The Harry-and-Louise ads were paid for by the Health Industry Association of America. The HIAA represents small and medium-sized insurance companies, which did indeed stand to lose business as a result of the Clinton plan—to the five largest companies, Aetna, Prudential, Cigna, Metropolitan Life, and the Travelers. As the Prudential executive quoted by Melvin Konner made clear, Prudential had little difficulty with the Clinton proposal; it and all the other big companies, save the Travelers, had always pushed for managed care and had helped finance the research of the Jackson Hole Group, an organization of policy experts that had broadly conceived a managed competition plan on which the Clinton proposal was in good part based. The Clintons strove, in light of the famous ads, to portray themselves as embattled slayers of the insurance dragon, but it just didn't sell. Of course, the Republicans were typically tenacious in their attacks on the Clinton plan, and the proposal also was roughed up a bit in the press, particularly in an oddly influential article in *The New Republic*, which seemed to win people over simply by virtue of the fact that its author had evidently read the 1,364-page document.

By the summer of 1994, the House Ways and Means Committee had passed a bill that was basically the Clinton plan, along with some elements of the more conservative bill offered by Tennessee Congressman Jim Cooper. For single-payer advocates, it did include an option for states to try their own single-payer plans, but that victory was somewhat undermined by a provision allowing large employers (those with 5,000 employees or more) to opt out. The Senate passed a much more incremental bill, which sought to cover 95 percent of Americans by the year 2002 and would have set up a commission to make recommendations if—when—that goal was not met. The House Education and Labor Committee voted out the McDermott bill, but only barely: by a vote of 22 to 21, it sent it to the floor without recommendation, a stipulation committees make when they want it known that they find a piece of legislation distasteful or difficult in some way. The vote was permitted by the chairman, William Ford, only on the condition that the 15 single-payer supporters on the committee vote for the compromise version of Clinton's bill.

Neither bill ever made it to a floor vote. For the single-payers, it was a defeat that, though hard to take, had to have been expected; for Clinton, it was one of the true low points of his presidency. His failure to get a health bill passed probably had plenty to do with the Democrats' humiliation at the polls four months later, which, in turn, has forced a series of events that makes the possibility of any kind of progressive resurgence seem remote. Probably not the way Bill Clinton wanted to be remembered.

Could the Clintons have passed a single-payer plan? It's doubtful. It did require a tax increase, and a big one. Of course, those taxes would have replaced insurance premiums, and that could have been explained, but opponents would still have had a field day with television commercials about that one. On the other hand, all of single-payer's advantages would undeniably have had wide appeal and would certainly have been much easier for people to grasp than the Clinton plan. It's true that a single-payer ballot initiative in California in 1994 lost badly— by 59 to 41 percent. But a group of underfinanced public interest lobbies trying to do something is one thing; a piece of federal legislation with the full support of the president is quite another.

There are two supposedly axiomatic truths about people's opinion of government that a vigorous debate on a single-payer plan would have brought to a head-on collision. First, that people hate big government. Second, that people hate big lobbies and vested interests. Single-payer would, without question, involve the government more fully in health care coverage and policy. However, it would also strike terror into two of the largest and most powerful lobbies in Washington: the doctors and the large insurers. So the political gamble would have come down to whether people would roll the dice on a government program that whacked the stuffing out of two powerful lobbying groups.

It's hard to say how it might've washed out. But consider the fact that people always say they'd be willing to pay more taxes if they were sure those taxes went to a specific good in which they could be certain to share. Consider also that this particular good, health care, is one that people have repeatedly said they want in better and more certain supply than they have now. Furthermore, single-payer could be combined with other offerings—like a general tax cut for middle- and low-income people, or some form of relief for small businesses—that would make the tax aspect less onerous. Given all these factors, people might have defied the experts and said yes to just this one government program. Opponents would have had their ad campaigns about new taxes, but imagine the single-payer ads featuring stogie-chomping insurance executives fretting about having to sell the yacht. And if the people hadn't gone for it, at least we'd know precisely where we stand. As it is, with the Clintons' bill, we know no more about what people want and don't want in health care reform than we knew before.

As I said above, a valid criticism of the left's attempt to sell the plan is that there was too much emphasis on the uninsured and not enough on the people, especially working par-

ents, who have insurance but are terrified that they'll lose it next week. This is a political choice rather than a moral one; no one's saying the uninsured don't matter but simply that, as a political calculation, the arguments should address those who are worried about losing their coverage. The inability—or unwillingness—to do so reflects a problem that I've tried to point out throughout this book: the left has no middle-class constituency anymore, and until it finds a way to reconnect with one, it's going to lose all these big fights.

A New York congressman told me a story on a different topic that is apposite. One day about 15 years ago, progressive New Yorkers gathered to decide how federal funds given under a particular housing program ought to be used. Practically everyone there wanted all the money to go to low-income housing. This congressman suggested that 15 percent or so should be set aside for middle-income subsidies, because if middle-income people were given at least a small stake in the program, its constituency would be more powerful politically. Naturally, he was upbraided, cursed, and called a moderate. But he was right as rain. Politicians are terrified of middle-class wrath and are far less likely to cut programs that serve the middle class—if they do, they lose votes doing it. While Republican politicians are destroying programs for the poor, they're moving much more cautiously on programs that affect the middle class—and as we saw in the Medicare debate, the GOP effort to rework that middle-class program appears to have cost the party support. As to the housing program in New York, the congressman lost the argument and said he was certain then that the program would eventually face the knife, as indeed it now does. The lesson is not to abandon the poor, obviously, but to bring the interests of poor people and middle-class people together as much as possible.

Back to single-payer. To sell the program in the future, there ought to be a little less talk about Canada, which, Neil

Young notwithstanding, does not impress many Americans as a place from which we need to import things. Single-payer should also be adapted to meet certain American needs and expectations, and thus make it less pervious to the standard criticisms. Specialty care and technological innovation, for example, which America does seem to do better than Canada, are real concerns. Finally, people who can afford it and want it must be able to buy supplemental insurance, and that should be a clear part of the plan. Some single-payer advocates oppose this, but it seems to me obvious that a $110,000-a-year family of four will never be sold on a plan that limits them to the same treatment that a $35,000-a-year family of four gets. This does not mean creating class divisions; just the opposite. If the $110,000 household and the $35,000 household both support the plan, cross-class solidarity has been created, with the middle class and the poor (or nearly poor) united. And by all means, make alliances that reach beyond the expected quarters. Ralph Nader, GM's Jack Smith, and representatives of the College of Surgeons, up on a stage together with a supportive president, would have far more impact on the public than Ralph Nader and four lesser goo-goos.

Single-payer has potential, then, not just as a health care fixative, but as a program that can bring the middle class and the poor, black and white, into a political coalition. It can help build a coalition that would turn the politics of the last 25 years on its head. There are prerequisites to doing so, however, that many on the left will find too difficult or else deny. In the next and final chapter, I'll discuss what those are, and suggest a general program for a new left (but not a New Left, because that's now an Old Left) that can accomplish this.

Chapter 8

THE LONG ROAD BACK

I n his short story "Edward and God," Milan Kundera, describing the constant human need to be reassured of one's beliefs, writes of the notion of "substitute fronts." When a movement that brings social or political upheaval reaches a climactic point, those within it take great pride in knowing that they're "on the correct side of the front lines." But time passes; the front lines shift or grow obscure, and with that comes the dissolution of the correct side. So people set up new, substitute, fronts to bring the correct side back into sharp relief, so that they may stand once again at the ramparts and keep alive the "habitual and precious sense of their own superiority."

Kundera's climactic point is the Communist takeover of the former Czechoslovakia and, as he hates nothing more than to be thought of as a political novelist, I note that the passage is only an aside. But he renders in a few paragraphs the same phenomenon that this book has sought to describe. When the

New Left was at its zenith, there was indeed a front and a correct side: the side of liberation and freedom that would show a complacent, self-satisfied, and conformity-rewarding society that underneath its ideal of the prosperous, middle-class, suburban life there churned a maelstrom of unresolved issues and unattended sicknesses.

Today, though, that front has dissolved. It is not that racism, sexism, homophobia, and other forms of prejudice don't exist, but rather that the demand for legal rights and recognition, around which the New Left movements were centered, has by now been carried about as far as it will go, about as far as it *can* go without disrupting civic culture and helping to spur the powerful backlash we see all around us. But those who need to reassure themselves of their superiority refuse to see the connection between disruption and backlash, and so new fronts are constantly established: the right of teenagers to make children; the idea of the anachronistic desuetude of the border; the insistence on diversity, whatever the means or consequences; the captious isolation of the angry white male. To these demands—as wrongheaded as they may be, at least they raise some pungent questions—one must add the less serious manifestations, because they too are fronts: the pursuit of hate speech laws, the policing of language, the brief of the federal government and women's legal groups against the Hooters restaurant chain. (If you don't like public television or gangsta rap or Robert Mapplethorpe's pictures, says today's left, just turn it off, don't listen to it, and don't go see them; but *we* don't like women showing off their breasts while they sling hamburgers, so you can't see them.)

The tactics, rather than advancing the front, have only retarded it. Similarly, the strategies that once helped advance the front, strategies the left still employs, don't have the impact today that they once did. In the 1960s, the protest march and demonstration had the ability to shock, awaken, and galvanize.

Nothing like the great civil rights marches had happened before in modern America; for many reporters based in New York and Washington, it was probably the first time they'd seen the Deep South or been forced to give hard thought to their country and the tarnished nature of its freedoms. Their sympathetic accounts conveyed that movement's righteousness and helped give it momentum. By now, television has so swallowed up such images as to make them indistinguishable from the many others that float into our homes. Today, a demonstration, no matter how large, is in many ways a quaint, perfunctory event, plotted for television and duly given its 45 seconds on the local news in between a shooting in a black neighborhood and a charity event in a white one, just another piece of aural and visual wallpaper that fades into a jumbled farrago of forgotten, and forgettable, images. The Million Man March proved a bit of an exception because the sight of several hundred thousand black men gathered in Washington *was* new, but it too faded away. Such events today lack the freshness and moral urgency they carried then.

The front today is elsewhere; but where? In Chapter One, I quoted the remark of scholar Henry Louis, Gates, Jr., apropos those who argue in favor of hate speech laws, that "generals are not the only ones who are prone to fight the last war." Gates's argument was that if the goals are the advance of freedom and opportunity and the end of bigotry, perhaps there exist better ways, in the 1990s, to reach them than those suggested by the hate speech activists. Gates wondered whether "the continuing economic and material inequality between black America and white America" could really be "treated simply through better racial attitudes." And he suggested that current economic conditions, which are really at the root of the crisis of black America—and, I would argue, the crisis of America as a whole—might be better addressed by finding

"new and subtler modes of economic analysis" and not by creating "new and subtler definitions of racism."

In a world in which the unchecked spread of global capitalism is all but inevitable, today's war is, at bottom, about jobs,
wages, and security. Fluid capital sees no color; to it, American
workers and their families, white, black, or otherwise, are expensive and thus must be circumvented and shortchanged
whenever possible—not because bosses or corporations are
immoral, but because it's logical for them to do so in order to
meet their needs (low production expenses, profit). And to
the extent that white working people are affected, does it not
make plain sense for the left to execute a strategy that includes
them as partners? Since our present-day condition of scarcity
began in 1973, the first post-war year in which wages stag-
nated, the country has been engaged in class warfare. But it
hasn't been working people against the owning class—instead,
it's been the other way around. And rights-based identity politics only makes matters worse. Working whites and blacks and
others cannot connect economically if they don't connect culturally, if there isn't some kind of common civic ballast to hold
them together.

If the left is to have any sort of power in this age, the first
thing that has to happen is for this thinking to change. The
particularist left must make peace with universalism, and the
fragmentary cultures the left now celebrates as oppositional or
transgressive must be reimagined and molded into a common
culture that can elevate society and change peoples' lives.

It's the fashion within today's left to scorn democracy and
reason and progress as "big, shaggy ideas," in the phrase of the
writer Katha Pollitt, that have run their course and been exposed for the hoaxes they are. Criticisms like Pollitt's amount to
an attack on the Enlightenment, the movement that advanced

the notions of rights and reason and secular anti-authoritarianism; that, as Kant put it, induced "the liberation of man from his self-caused state of minority" and united people beyond their cultures and identities. As I noted in the introduction, rationalistic Enlightenment thinking does have its limitations, and it's true that some who invoke its tenets today are merely calling for the reestablishment of the old relationships between the races and the sexes, or for a return to some kind of "simpler time" or "good old days" that did not, for many people, exist.

But if democracy and reason have run their course, what exists to replace them? To this question, the left has not produced an answer that comes close to meeting people's needs. The only answer the left has posited is biology as destiny. Philosophically, it's an answer that's about as useful as the prelapsarian myths of the Bible; politically, it's an answer that is doing the ruling class' work for it.

The left needs, then, to do two things: first, to recapture the Enlightenment belief in universal human beings with universal rights and wrest that belief out of the conservatives' hands into the possession of a renewed movement that envisions democracy and reason not as dead ends but as unfinished works that can and must be improved; and second, to mediate fixed identities by a more ready recognition of fluid ones, to develop an ethos that will be more willing to accept definitions of people other than those of race, ethnicity, gender, and sexual orientation. A recognition, in other words, that we must respect group identities, but we must do so by conceiving of affiliations among people that stretch beyond those categories. I have tried to demonstrate throughout this book that the left is getting pounded by the right on the issues I discussed because of our reflexive reliance on a shriveling coalition of out-groups whose demands have nothing to do with a larger concern for our common humanity and every-

thing to do with a narrow concern for fragmented and supposedly oppositional cultures. Only through a more majoritarian politics, which recognizes that people have many destinies
other than the ones birth assigns to them and many affiliations
and obligations beyond their group, can the left regain the
ground it has lost in recent years.

The emancipatory potential of reason and knowledge has
been affirmed by many thinkers, most notably the philosopher Jürgen Habermas. He has argued that reason and
knowledge can lead to power, which is not, as the postmodernists would have it, some arbitrary and capricious thing
that seeps inexorably like a gas into every crevice of life, but
is based on real social conditions that can be changed. The
historian John Patrick Diggins suspects, and I think correctly,
that much of today's left takes a perverse comfort in its powerlessness, in being chained to despair's coffle—after all,
when one's decisions have few actual consequences, one
can do whatever one pleases. He argues that the left, rather
than throw up its collective hands because power is immut-
able and mysterious, must figure out ways to seize it: "Power
is not some alien presence contrary to nature. It is intrinsic
to the very constitution of men and women contending with
the conditions of history. Poststructuralist philosophers have
only described a world supposedly lost to the concealed
structures of domination. The challenge the left faces is not
to despair about power but to uncover its hidden operations
in order to control it better with countervailing mechanisms." To this challenge, Diggins asserts, the Enlightenment—particularly as its ideas were advanced in America—
"remains directly relevant." Diggins argues that the work of
America's founders, the pragmatist philosopher John Dewey,
and Karl Marx shows how "knowledge joined to power" is
the precondition of freedom, and that it's up to people to

fuse them instead of bewailing a world "lost to the concealed structures of domination."

Certainly it is the tendency among the left's out-groups to "despair about power" and complain that oppression is so overwhelmingly present in every aspect of life that the only possible liberatory strategy is to point this out over and over again wherever it's found—hence, the always widening search for "new and subtler" -isms. One cannot reasonably deny that oppression still exists, at times quite brutally, but neither can one reasonably suggest that things are no better than they were 30 or 60 or 90 years ago. Things are in many ways better and in some ways worse, and this contradiction is the very essence of modern life.

But modernity's relationship to progressive change is very real indeed—it's only through gaining knowledge that people over time learn to reason for themselves. Furthermore, America's philosophical commitment to universal rights, equality, and emancipation is real too. This is not to say that slavery and Jim Crow are to be treated as mere aberrations. They are central to American history, but so are the Emancipation Proclamation and the rise of labor and the civil rights laws of the '60s. There has always been a tension: between the originally stated commitment to freedom and the three-fifths clause, between the Warren and the Rehnquist courts. The left's task is not to use the clause and the Rehnquist court's decisions as evidence of bad faith. Rather, its task has always been to test the claim that the commitment is real. That's what the labor movement did, it's what the civil rights movement did. But in the last 25 or so years, the left has spent far less energy making good-faith efforts to test that claim than it has finding ways to prove its self-fulfilling, and self-defeating, point that the claim is a ruse. Jefferson owned slaves; Jefferson was the chief architect of the American ideals of equality and freedom. Which Jefferson is relevant to us today? I'm afraid the recent left, with its small-minded fixation on dead white males, has answered the question as glumly and incorrectly as it can possibly be answered.

How can the left conceive this new common good? In essence, by conceding an individual's multiple identities, by expressing a vision of society in which people are recognized as having the ability—and the right—to transcend the identities the left wishes to assign them and call themselves whatever they please.

The historian David A. Hollinger has identified the tension between such identities as a tension between pluralism, which he traces to the American philosopher Horace Kallen, and cosmopolitanism, which has its roots in the writings of his counterpart and better-known contemporary, Randolph Bourne. Both, Hollinger writes, believed in what we today call multiculturalism, but whereas Kallen's pluralism argued for group autonomy and resistance to assimilation, Bourne's cosmopolitanism envisioned a nation in which an individual's group affiliation was a matter not just of biology but of consent—the difference between involuntary and voluntary affiliation. It has to be noted that cosmopolitanism is scarcely a word that should be used as a rallying cry, given its historic anti-Semitic connotation and its certain lack of appeal to ordinary working people. But whatever it should be called, it's a healthy urge. Hollinger calls for a "post-ethnic" worldview that prefers "voluntary to prescribed affiliations, appreciates multiple identities, pushes for communities of wide scope, recognizes the constructed character of ethno-racial groups, and accepts the formation of new groups as a part of the normal life of a democratic society." The individual is *both* a member of a group, whose interests will at times take precedence, and, in Enlightenment tradition, a universal human being with rights and obligations and affiliations beyond the group.

Such a human being can reason on his or her own terms. Group affiliations are easy. One connects with those like oneself, whether the category is racial, sexual, or even regional, on an emotional level. To connect with those unlike oneself, to overcome the mistrust of the new and different that is, unfortunately, built into all of us, requires reason. Newt Gingrich and other conservatives can use emotional appeals to make the rest of the country hate New York City; when reason prevails, Georgians and New Yorkers understand that they are not each other's enemy. A universal person whose affiliations are voluntary, at least in part, can and must make decisions that rise above emotional appeals to sameness. The *nonpersonal* is political—as it must be.

What this can mean, in real political terms, includes but is not limited to the following: we find smarter ways to spend our energies than finding bigots under every bed; there are no litmus tests for black authenticity, such as supporting Louis Farrakhan or Leonard Jeffries, or, for that matter, for white authenticity; a straight white male is not immediately suspect if, say, he opposes affirmative action; we can talk about the problem of welfare not only as a function of race- and gender-based oppression, but as a problem that has behavioral attributes that must be addressed; we can discuss illegal immigration similarly; the white working class is not some totemic object of derision and contempt, but comprises actual human beings who can be appealed to as a possible source of cooperation and power; we can even revive the notion of a working-class culture that leaps over ethnic and racial boundaries and that provides common points of reference, and comfort, for disparate workers; enemies and allies of progressive thought can be identified and named as they really stand and not as a function of the ticket they hold in the multicultural sweepstakes; finally, people can express legitimate disagreement with a group line without being automatically accused of some kind of -ism.

I believe that people across the country are desperate to rise out of the quicksand of current political categories, desperate for an idea of community that lays waste to both inflexible left-wing multiculturalism and right-wing divide and conquer. Community, here, means connectedness based not on personal acquaintance but on a shared understanding—what one might call civic empathy—of people who live across town, or in another state, who have problems similar to one's own. It explicitly means affiliations across racial and religious lines, made voluntarily by people on both sides because they see that, whatever their differences, they share experiences and dilemmas, and such affiliations can provide comfort and succor (to say nothing of political strength). It means having faith—not naive faith, but a faith rooted in history and reason—in people and in the principle that democracy is still ours to mold. The right claims that it is creating such a community, but most people know intuitively that it is not. It is, in fact, ruling through a creaky coalition held together by the assumption that the white working and middle classes, provided they're kept in an agitated state about the culture, will continue to accept their small piece of the pie. If the left can develop a rhetoric that conquers that thinking, it will begin to succeed in creating a transcendent politics of real multiculturalism that rises above cultural rigidities; a politics that this nation of diverse and similar people deserves.

Isn't this how life really is? Our language, customs, and literature; our art, architecture, and sculpture; our food, clothes, and popular music—all are a product of the great melange of cultures that have created, and continue to create, the American nation. It's time our politics caught up. For the left, it means relaxing the standard of authenticity down to a level that is more tolerant, more open to iconoclasm and differences of opinion (the great paradox: the politics of difference ends up tolerating so little difference), more willing to subject itself to debate and analysis. Will people on the left be willing to relax their defensive posture, a posture taken partly in response to the right's ascendance, just as the right appears to be at its zenith? The answer is, they must; it's the only way out. Trying to perfect the opposite tendencies—to close debate, to avoid nettlesome counterarguments, to hold intolerant standards of authenticity—will kill off the left and hopelessly divide the country. Too much time has already been wasted by those now making such demands, people who, as the critic Marshall Berman put it, "rest content in the artificial inner light of their inflated domes." It is well past time that the domes be lifted.

As I said above, changing such thinking is only the *first* thing that has to be done if the left is to thrive again. Even if all the questions of philosophy and ideology were settled tomorrow, something would still be needed: a program. Here, I suggest some guiding principles and some possible policies that keep in mind the goal of creating a program that adheres to the fore-going tenets, tries to talk to regular people about their con-cerns, and has the potential to build a new coalition that will render obsolete those described by today's politics. I will ar-range my suggestions according to four broadly defined policy areas: jobs and security; democracy; personal liberty; and civic community.

The first principle of a new left program is to fight the new war: to produce a strategy to protect working families in the age of globalization. Millions of Americans are terrified as never before that they won't have a job next week, or that their health insurance will be cancelled or reduced, and with good reason: from 1979 to 1992, Fortune 500 companies ter-minated nearly 4.5 million workers, and NAFTA, by several estimates, has already shipped more than 500,000 jobs south. Some congressional Democrats and a few Republicans have resisted this trend, but it's fair to say that both major parties are standing on the sidelines whistling while this goes on, if not actively encouraging it.

Trade agreements like NAFTA are probably inevitable; better than fighting them, the left should push for the inclusion of provisions like an equalization tax on certain imports, so that goods made cheaply in the Third World cannot be imported to undersell the same goods that are made here more expensively. Trade agreements must also include trade union and environmental riders that seek to establish some semblance of rights for workers in the trading countries. Just as importantly, we need to create a rhetoric that shows how, as sociologist Charles Derber writes, "the crisis of values begins among elites who preach community but undermine it in the service of power and money," and how "family values and community morality depend on a new economy that takes stock of the social consequences of business decisions." Someone—preferably a president, and preferably someone other than Pat Buchanan—has to be willing to reproach U.S. corporations publicly, and regularly, for the ways in which they're failing the people who depend on them. The idea that an American CEO makes 45 times the wage of the average employee is preposterous, and the idea that men who bring their companies to the cusp of ruin are actually rewarded with golden parachute severance deals is sickening.

Such is the reality of the sound-bite age that only when a presidential candidate or a party leader or some other major figure says this, and says it repeatedly, will these conditions begin to change. And the rhetoric has to be aimed at galvanizing working people around a positive idea—the potential they have as political partners to make corporations and politicians respond to them—and not a negative one (that they should resent these rich white men who'll never change). That candidate or party must be willing to forgo those CEOs' donations, but the working people of this country are surely desperate for a political leader to say some of these things. Imagine a president saying, on the occasion of something like the merger of Chase Manhattan and Chemical banks, which will render "redundant" some 12,000 workers, that such a transaction is unethical, and meeting with some of the 12,000. And imagine him doing these kinds of things on a regular basis instead of once in a while for the sake of a photo-op. The mood in this country would change.

The left must advance a serious program of workers' protections. The presumption has always been in this country that the economy would find new work for the thousands tossed out in mergers or displaced by technology. But, as the author Jeremy Rifkin has argued, that's less and less true. If it's true that there may be less work in the future, how do we handle that? Rifkin is so bold as to have proposed consideration of the 30-hour workweek—it may sound laughable at first blush, but it's a time-honored idea that briefly had a real shot at becoming law in the 1930s; FDR later expressed regret that he scuttled it in favor of the National Industrial Recovery Act.

The argument, in an era of ever-increasing technological unemployment, is for more workers to do in 30 hours a week the jobs that fewer workers now do in 40 hours a week. Such an arrangement should result in large productivity gains for employers in which workers would end up sharing, giving more families more collective purchasing power. Some companies tried it in the 1930s, like the Kellogg cereal company, and reported reduced overhead costs, lower job-related injury rates, and much higher productivity and employment rates. This might mean less income for some, depending on how much a business saved in productivity and related costs, but it would also mean more leisure time for all—a three-day weekend—and a stronger, healthier life within the community, a trade-off that some people, particularly second wage earners, would find appealing. In any event, if the choice were between layoffs and restructured hours, surely most workers would take the latter.

In several Western European countries, as the academic Stanley Aronowitz has pointed out, public sector shrinkage has been handled not through layoffs as they have in America but by giving employees the option of a four-day week. The move toward a shorter workweek need not begin with federal legislation; perhaps a few creative union and management relationships around the country could experiment with such programs (certainly, it's a way for unions to retain and even increase membership). Indeed, the left should probably emphasize nonlegislative approaches in more areas—local experiments, which, if they worked well, could serve as models for national action.

The issue of more leisure time, in an age in which family structure is changing so rapidly, is a vital one. Historically (although not lately), American productivity has been geared toward producing a higher standard of living and more consumer spending, but today, like Alice at the Red Queen's command, people are running faster just to stay in the same place. Will people accept a slightly less get-ahead, consumer-driven society in exchange for more leisure time? Many of them may, especially overworked parents who do what they can to watch their children grow but realize they're missing some of life's sweetest moments. Shorter hours, part-time and flex-time arrangements, work out of the home; all these are potentially political issues that the left should press. And why is it that among the advanced nations, the United States gives its workers the least time off? Workers in most European countries have three or four weeks paid vacation. The reason we don't have such arrangements here is not that they're somehow "alien" to the American character; the reason is that we've got two political parties that don't care that employees don't have them and unions too crippled, corrupt, and frozen in time to imagine demanding them.

Workers should have more say over how their companies are run and how their pensions are invested. This has happened in certain instances, most notably at Weirton Steel in West Virginia, where workers are now fully involved decision-makers and stockholders. After careening into near bankruptcy, Weirton Steel has made a comeback. Reforms that would bind a company more directly to the people and community it serves could help ensure longer-lasting relationships. Corporations today get tax breaks for contributing to their employees' retirement, through 401K plans and other such programs. How about setting up similar structures that would help employees save for a down payment on a home or for their children's college education? And on-site day care should be a mandatory feature of every large workplace in America, financed through employer and employee contributions. For everyone else, government-supervised and privately run day-care centers, paid for from general revenues and monthly fees paid by parents, are clearly needed. Parental leave after the birth of a child should also be mandatory—three months paid, with options for more time unpaid. Once again, they do it everywhere else in the advanced world. Finally, the left must create some salable version of single-payer health care, administered not in Washington but primarily at the state or even local level.

Where does the money come from? The answers I offer are not new ones, but that doesn't make them any less valid. We do not need a $240 billion Pentagon budget, and we do not need $1 billion B-2 bombers (the entire cost of AFDC, remember, is equal to the cost of about 15 such bombers; right now, we have 20, and we're building 20 more). I doubt that most people really feel we need 40 of them. They have voted for the party that says we need them, not because of that issue. In a post-Cold War era, the right will have a hard time keeping alive a rationale for hawkish defense spending. Of course, job loss in the defense industry is a problem that has to be reckoned with. But there's no lack of conversion plans; there's just a lack of political will to get on with them.

There is also the corporate welfare issue. The libertarian Cato Institute has identified $85 billion in such government subsidies to some of the largest corporations in the country (which are also, of course, some of the largest campaign contributors). This is waste that the Republican "attack" on corporate welfare, which is advanced purely for the sake of perceptions, hardly touches. If that $85 billion were retrieved, there'd be no need for cuts in Head Start, Medicare and Medicaid would be fine, and there'd probably be some left over. There is also the fact that corporations pay a far smaller share of the national tax bill in general than they did 40 years ago— 38 percent then, 13 percent now. Forcing corporate taxes up is probably a less wise strategy than forcing corporations to contribute to employees' welfare in the various ways discussed above, but in either case, their contribution to the general weal would increase. And if we must talk of individual and family tax cuts, let's make them for middle-class and poor people—individuals from, say, $50,000 down, families from $80,000 down, or the like, giving slightly greater relief to the poorest earners.

I'll save more details for the economists. In short, and as everyone knows intuitively, the money is there. But let's remember: class-based economic politics can't succeed without an accompanying class politics of culture. This doesn't mean lining up people to sing the *Internationale*; it means doing all the things I described earlier in this chapter, and elsewhere, to make working blacks and whites, men and women, $80,000-a-year accountants and $20,000-a-year orderlies, feel they have a stake in something together.

Second: governmental reform. It's often been said that nothing can change in this country until the nexus of money and politics is crushed, and it's clearly true. I'd have put governmental reform first on my list except that I believe that jobs and security are the central issues for any kind of left coalition building, whereas government reform is not just a left-wing program these days (n.b., the Perotistas).

The ideas are already out there, and for the most part, they're good ones. Limits on soft money, especially, are vital, soft money being the huge cash contributions—well above the limit that people can donate to candidates—that individuals can make to parties, and that parties in turn throw toward their candidates. Free television time for candidates is a must, as are shorter campaign seasons and weekend elections in which the polls are open both Saturday and Sunday. Restrictions on gifts and honoraria are useful, as are more stringent disclosure requirements.

To these, let me add a suggestion that may sound a tad gimmicky but that strikes right at the heart of things. The problem is that politicians receive their contributions and the voters never really have a chance to know about them. If you're a voter and you see that your congressman came out against something opposed by the American Medical Association, and you're wondering how much money from the A.M.A. and from individual doctors your congressman has received, you cannot find out. The documents are available of course, but if you're an average person who has more pressing things to do than spend hours researching the matter, you'll never know. And you can't depend on the media or your local Naderites to do it, because the media usually are not very interested and the Naderites are continually pressed for time and funds.

Why not, then, a people's clearinghouse to answer such questions? Either with a phone call or over your computer, you can get specific answers to specific questions about money and legislation. Did the trial lawyers host a fund raiser for your congressman? How did he vote on legislation ATLA was interested in? Did he speak before the trial lawyers? How much insurance money has he received, or National Rifle Association money, and what action has he taken on their bills, from committee markup to floor vote? The "good" lobbyists, the public interest lobbies and such, will never have the money to neutralize the oil and chemical lobbyists, or the National Association of Manufacturers; so you neutralize their money in another way, by making it less mysterious, making it as easy for people to find out about lobbyists' money as it is for them to check their own bank balances. If members of Congress knew people could watch them that closely, they'd be far more careful about how they operate. Needless to say, the clearinghouse should monitor not just members of Congress, but presidents as well.

Congress, of course, would not be likely to fund such an animal, and it probably should not even be trusted to Congress to set it up, because if it is, inevitably there will be loopholes. It should be set up privately. And let the people fund it—the institutions that profess an abiding interest the public good, like media organizations, foundations, charitable trusts, the Ross Perots, and finally the rest of us, with $25 or $50 donations (or whatever) made the way we make them to public television or wildlife funds or what have you. Even a small fee per call—but small enough that it's not a barrier, say $2—appended to one's monthly phone bill is not unreasonable.

Of course, such a clearinghouse would be used by activists on the right as well, and there's a risk that it might augment their influence. But for every $1,000 a politician takes from, say, a gay rights group, she or he takes many thousands from the interests that lobby for corporate agendas. The weight of evidence, in other words, will support our side. It's up to the left to make noise about the right things.

There is much delusion around the idea of reforming Congress and lessening the influence of money in Washington. Even if every good government reform ever proposed were adopted, things still wouldn't change as much as reformers believe. The clearinghouse idea has the benefit of not relying on the phony hope of changing Washington's habits; instead, it relies on arming people with loads of information, which, on this particular topic, is exactly what politicians don't want them to have. Habits will change.

Third: personal liberty. Conservatives are right to say that statist liberalism has in some respects intruded into people's private space. Of course, conservatives do it too, in other areas, but don't like to admit it. After the 1994 elections, the writer Christopher Hitchens was, so far as I know, the first leftist to observe that the left should forge a "new synthesis" with libertarianism. So let's allow for a quasilibertarian perspective that banishes both liberal and conservative forms of intrusion and gives people the right to live their lives however they see fit, up to the point where their actions affect the well-being of others.

A woman's right to choose abortion is an issue of personal liberty; I needn't spend much more time on that since it's one of the few stands of the left that most of the general public supports. Even if the Supreme Court strikes down *Roe v. Wade*, it will probably do so not by outlawing abortion outright but by returning the issue to the states, and many states will pass abortion rights laws. Gay civil rights are also a matter of personal liberty. A long-term goal should be the addition to federal civil rights law of protection against discrimination based on sexual orientation. That may be some time in coming: it won't be popular, opposition will be thunderous, and it may undo the very coalition this book seeks to build. A more majoritarian approach to gay rights, and one that fits nicely into a left-libertarian schema, may be the legitimation of gay marriage. Gay people would thus have the right to live without fear of state encroachment on personal decisions, and the fact that the demand would be based on extension of an already respected institution might mollify some conservative opposition. David Boaz of the libertarian Cato Institute has eloquently championed this cause, and it even has some conservative defenders, like the editors of *The Economist* and former Bush administration adviser James Pinkerton.

The broader gay identity agenda is another matter and, as should be clear from my discussion of identity politics, I do think that some aspects of that agenda and its strategies are fractious and have sometimes been advanced with the specific intent of alienating working-class people. Rainbow curricula in the schools, for example, are not worth the turmoil they cause. Children should learn tolerance *in the home* before we worry about their learning it in the schools. Accomplishing that means building a society based on mutual tolerance. It's a much bigger job than roping a few school board liberals into signing on to another social program, but it's the real work that has to be done; anything less is a smokescreen, and parents see right through it—not because they're homophobic, but because they're wary, as well they should be, of liberal elites lecturing them on yet another way they can improve themselves.

Personal liberty means at least two more things. First, profound respect for the Bill of Rights and a stance of principled (but not zealous) civil libertarianism. Out with hate speech and bias crime and antipornography crusades. And, while we're defending amendments, let's not exclude the Second. It is time, in other words, to rethink gun control. I live in a city with perhaps the strictest gun laws in the nation; it is also bursting with firearms of every imaginable sort. I don't doubt that some deaths do occur that might not have happened otherwise because a gun was handy, but is the carnage in our streets at its root a function of guns? It's a function of poverty, of the existence of a class of people, especially teenage boys and young men, who've been left to fend for themselves and told in every possible way that society has no use for them and would sooner they mow one another down than pay the cost of processing and jailing them. As long as they exist, they'll have guns, legally or illegally. As long as drug cartels exist, they'll have guns too. Besides, guns are a vice, and people like their vices and will always take considerable risks to procure them—witness the drug trade. Meanwhile, what about the hunters, collectors, and target shootists? It's obviously very important to them, and it's no harm to anyone else, so give them what they want. Tighter restrictions on gun *selling* make sense—right now, it's far easier to set up shop as a firearms seller than it is to start a McDonald's; there are more "gun shops," which literally can consist of a person in an apartment with a suitcase full of revolvers, than there are gas stations in America. But as for law-abiding individuals, let them have their guns, even their assault weapons; move this issue down on the list of things to worry about and watch, incidentally, as the National Rifle Association's position diminishes.

Finally, personal liberty means respecting the fact that people want as little state interference in their lives as possible. The state cannot tell a woman when to bear a child, and it can't peep in a gay person's bedroom or a hunter's gun closet. More than that, the government cannot be some big national nanny (the coinage is the journalist Nicholas von Hoffman's, in another context) minding the children. This is how some liberals, the antitobacco-crusading California Congressman Henry Waxman being the prime example, see the state; this should not be, however, the viewpoint of the left, which by contrast should seek a state that arms people with political and economic rights but otherwise gives them freedom to live as they like. If people want to smoke, drink, or eat themselves to death, the government has little business interfering with their progress, provided, of course, that they're harming no one else. By all means, continue smoking education and go after the tobacco companies' ludicrously generous federal subsidies, the reduction of which would serve many good purposes. But don't attack people's behavior. In a similar vein, federal regulations should stop at the point where they impinge upon decisions that are obviously private (e.g., the way wetlands regulations sometimes affect small landowners) or just don't serve any real purpose. Reviewing such regulations for overreach should emphatically be the left's business: bureaucracies do tend to impose rules simply to sustain their own reason for being, and I see no radical interest in supporting such impositions. Besides, as with larger issues addressed elsewhere in this book, leave such reviews to the right, and we know what happens.

Fourth: civic community. I would place under this heading much of the social policy that has occupied the bulk of this book and that claims a hold on so much of the national discourse. Issues, that is, on which one's position says much about one's view of what constitutes a just nation. My belief, which should be clear from the first part of this chapter, is that building a civic community is a function of a new way of thinking about how to create a politics that transcends fixed group interests. Nevertheless, as with anything, specific policy choices have to be made.

With respect to civil rights: instead of finding new and more elaborate ways to identify and punish racism, why don't we concentrate on enforcing the laws that are already on the books but are so weakly policed as to be rendered a joke? It's illegal for real estate agencies, for example, to discriminate on the basis of race. Yet they do it all the time. They get away with it because district attorneys and federal prosecutors don't regularly investigate such matters, and they don't investigate them because it's not an issue civil rights leaders press. But why not? Housing discrimination is one of the most omnipresent forms of bigotry in the country, particularly in large cities; its demise would mean a much more vigorously integrated society. Civil rights leaders would do far better to demand that local law enforcement agencies aggressively pursue this matter than they do by issuing press releases giving their opinion on the number of blacks governor so-and-so has named to his administration. And who could oppose such an effort? Some people might argue that they'd rather see the money spent fighting organized crime or what have you, but no one would dare oppose it on principle, since it's based on equality of opportunity and, as we saw in the affirmative action chapter, even Pat Buchanan now accepts that.

Bank lending is a similar issue, little discussed but absolutely pivotal in the lives of minority neighborhoods. This issue is at the heart of the the huge economic divide between white and black, but it ranks low on the civil rights agenda. Usually, in New York City at least, a certain community empowerment group puts out an annual report on lending discrimination. A civil rights spokesperson or two attends the press conference and that's it, a one-day story. I'm not blaming the group, but that's not enough. The Community Reinvestment Act, the federal law that requires banks to put money back in the communities they serve, is extremely weak and needs toughening. In addition, how about a civil rights insistence that state bank regulators hire more inspectors to police lending discrimination? Not as sexy as arguing about Farrakhan, I'll grant you, but probably more useful to more people. Pursuits like these, while bringing real relief to people, have the additional virtue of being grounded in principles—racial equality and fair treatment of all—around which consensus is overwhelming.

In general, the left needs to find ways to advance people's rights that don't seek to create confrontation and that don't reflexively assume that the more superficially radical and transgressive an idea sounds, the better. Some confrontation is unavoidable and desirable—for example, taxing wealthy people at a rate higher than they'd like is a desirable confrontation. But in other cases, I think ways can be found that will lessen social tensions and accomplish similar goals. Adding a class element to affirmative action may be one such way. Also, instead of lowering standards to help blacks and Latinos, more effort should be put into raising their abilities, as former schools chancellor Ramon Cortines did in New York City.

Racial redistricting serves a useful goal when it corrects a grotesque history of gerrymandering, by which black neighborhoods were divided into numerous legislative districts to erode black political power, as was routinely done in large cities. But must districts illogically snake halfway across a state, joining people on the basis of their racial identity but separating others whose identity as neighbors is disregarded? These districts' lack of geographic integrity is a perfect encapsulation of biological identity superseding all other forms. A side effect in the South, by the by, is that contiguous districts are increasingly electing Republicans, so that after one or two more censuses, if racial redistricting continues as is, we'll see nearly all the white South being represented by conservative Republicans, hopelessly isolating black people into a powerlessness not, in the final analysis, so different from the old days. There will be more black Democrats in Congress, but they'll be part of a shrinking, permanent, powerless minority.

Right now, so-called majority-minority districts are drawn so that blacks or Latinos or whomever make up 70 percent or more of the voting age population. Reducing that threshold to, say, 45 percent would still give minorities a reasonable shot at electing one of their own and preserve some measure of geographic integrity. It would also force an outcome in which the winner would prevail by collecting votes on a multiracial basis. Isn't that really what we want?

The left has thrown in with liberal statism largely as a defensive posture against the right's assaults on liberal legislation, but beyond that, there's no good reason for the left to be so heavily invested in it. Again, the right has a point, if for the wrong reasons: the federal government probably is not the right vehicle for achieving certain things, not (as the right says) because it's inefficient but because it's impersonal and inhuman. The left must conceive of ways to help the poor that go beyond government programs and that foster more community input and obligation. Make community service a component of a public education, even of higher education. Give tax or some other kind of relief to middle-class people who perform community service. Without removing federal commitments the way the right wants to, find ways to make welfare and illegitimacy not just federal responsibilties but local ones, neighborhood ones. Bring teenage mothers and their children under the sponsorship of stable families; pay the families a stipend to take them in and bonuses if the mother finishes school or job training; meanwhile, the children raised in that stability will show its effects. There is a downside to neighbors believing that providing for the poor is solely a federal responsibility and a salutary upside to instilling in those neighbors a sense of responsibility to be shared with a federal government that provides money and sets general guidelines or standards.

We also have to find practical ways for the poor and the middle class to make common cause—namely, by designing policies and programs that give both a stake. I'd go so far as to say that all poverty programs should give middle-class people a share of the pie. A housing program, as the New York congressman argued in the previous chapter, should send 15 or 20 percent of its money to middle-income people; likewise a home-care program, what have you. Politicians don't fear the poor; they fear middle-class voters. Programs with middle-class constituencies, even smallish ones, are far less likely to come under attack than programs with only poor constituencies.

I have not devoted much space to education because the ground has been so well trod in the culture wars. Progressives should continue to support efforts to include more in the textbooks about the lives and fates of slaves, American Indians, and others on the receiving end of American progress (let us not forget those abroad, from Filipinos to Greeks to Nicaraguans). But this history should be taught not out of pietistic concern for the self-esteem of minority children, as the left has posited, but simply because it is information that all American children, all future citizens, should have. And the left should be leading the push for higher academic standards, for more learning and reading. Those of us who hold radical analyses of the world didn't self-esteem our way to such positions; we read and we thought. Finally, the left should take the lead in advocating a longer school day and a longer school year, even more years of schooling. These will cost money, of course, but if parents and other taxpayers see a direct return on their investment—i.e., a stronger education for their children—they probably won't mind shelling out quite as much.

The above program is not, of course, a full platform. What I've tried to do is establish principles—community, civic feeling, tolerance, compromise, optimism—and give examples of ways that the left could build on those principles. To some readers, portions of the above may sound "conservative." Quite true, there are ideas here that don't suit the categories in which we've grown accustomed to think—which is precisely my point. Relying on those old categories, the left has been inspiring and reaching practically no one. What I've sketched above may not be the one and only cure-all, but I do know that it puts people's livelihoods first, not their fixed identities, and it places faith in ordinary people instead of holding them in contempt.

It's the basic rule of evolution: adapt, or die. It holds as true for political movements as it does for species. Left and right are simply no longer what they once were. The left has spent 25 years trying to etch perfect jewels out of categories that had real meaning in, say, 1970. Meanwhile, the world has changed. The left is emerging from its workshop to find that these etched jewels, no matter how perfectly shaped, don't fit anywhere. They don't fit because, while the left was in its workshop, everyone else was out in the world, changing it: the owners of capital, the conservative intellectuals, the dema-gogues, the militarists; they wrestled with the world's real con-ditions and remade it in the image they want. They did it, some of them, by making emotional appeals to people's worst instincts, and, through lies and false promises about things like tax cuts and supply-side economics. But we should be careful to note that that's not all they did. They were smart. And they had new ideas and pushed them with vigor, and they took every opening their limping opposition gave them. They adapted.

Yes, as I said above, the world has changed in good ways too, changes that emerged from the workshop. But those changes, as anyone watching knows well, have not meant tri-umph. They've come as a result of just trying to keep up. When a serial killer is apprehended and brought to justice, it's counted a great victory for the criminal justice investigators, and so it may be; but what about the dead bodies? The left can claim some victories in recent years. But what about the dead bodies? There are far, far too many of them, figuratively and literally, for the left to delude itself into thinking it has been an effective force.

And many of the carcasses belong to the people the left has allowed itself to lose faith in and forget about, the very people the left was born to represent and embrace. They are not perfect people; they certainly can't begin to meet the demands today's left would place on them. Like all people, they're both bad and good. We can help them, and they us, by showing that we care about their lives and have faith in them to behave like citizens, no more or less.

I've lived in two very different places for most of my life. But as dissimilar as West Virginia and New York City are, the people, in fundamental ways, are surprisingly alike. Social mores vary greatly, of course, but at bottom, people's lives, their concerns and hopes, are not so different. In my first journalism job in New York, as a reporter for one of the city's many small weeklies, I sat through endless, in both number and duration, community meetings. I remember being shocked, as they pored over the fine print of their many resolutions, that people in hypersophisticated and anything-goes Greenwich Village cared so deeply about the condition of the trees in front of their apartment buildings or about whether a cafe's signage was appropriate to the neighborhood. Later, when I'd spent more time in Harlem, I learned that people there care about the same things, and must tend to them, of course, against tougher odds than their counterparts downtown. The tomato plants one sometimes sees growing in the narrow patch of unfriendly earth deposited between the northbound and southbound lanes of Broadway in the Puerto Rican and Dominican neighborhoods of upper Manhattan may seem wildly incongruous to a rural reader, but to me, they say something about the common urges that people facing vastly different circumstances share; just like the gardeners living along Broadway, my parents and grandparents grew their own tomatoes, and it was a matter of great pride to have them ripen just so on the window sill and be ready for use in that night's salad.

I suppose people can grow gardens even under the worst of political conditions. But to miss the importance of such common desires, small and large, among tenement dwellers and suburbanites and farmers is to misunderstand an important part of what political movements are for: we seek to create them, in a nation of such immense diversity, so that people can feel a part of something bigger than themselves. Something hopeful and optimistic; something that tells people not to believe that they're mere subjects in a corrupt empire and that they should just be prepared for the worst. Something that reaches simultaneously into history and into the future. It shows them faces different from their own, but reassures them that the dreams behind those faces are like their own. From this stew emerges a common idea, about hope, about improving not only their own lives but the lives of others; about all of them being able to live their dreams. And that strikes me as a pretty good definition of justice.

INDEX

215